The Ultimate Tech Book for Beginners and Seniors (Large Print Edition)

Unlock the Power of Digital Tools

The Digital Grandson's Guide to Tech

Digital Grandson Press

The Ultimate Tech Book for Beginners and Seniors (Large Print Edition): Unlock the Power of Digital Tools

Copyright © 2024 Digital Grandson Press. All rights reserved.

No part of this publication may be reproduced, distributed, or transmitted in any form or by any means, including photocopying, recording, or other electronic or mechanical methods, without the prior written permission of the publisher, except in the case of brief quotations embodied in critical reviews and certain other noncommercial uses permitted by copyright law.

Publisher's Note

The information provided in this book is designed to be a helpful and informative guide for older adults learning to use technology. While the publisher and author have made every effort to ensure the information is accurate at the time of publication, technology is constantly evolving. Therefore, we cannot guarantee the completeness, accuracy, or timeliness of the contents.

Trademarks

Apple, Android, Google Maps, Amazon Echo, Alexa, and other trademarks are the property of their respective owners. The use of these trademarks is not intended to imply any affiliation with or endorsement by the respective companies.

ISBN: 9798346405306

First Edition

Disclaimers

This book is intended for educational purposes only. The publisher and the author make no representations or warranties with respect to the accuracy, applicability, fitness, or completeness of the contents of this book. The information contained in this book is strictly for educational purposes. Readers are advised to use their best judgment and consult with a professional for any specific concerns.

Portions of this book were created using AI tools, specifically to assist with drafting and editing. All content has been reviewed, edited, and approved by the author to ensure accuracy, clarity, and quality. The use of AI is intended to enhance the writing process and provide clear, easy-to-follow instructions.

Contents

Welcome — 1
    You're Not Alone
    The Purpose of This Book
    How This Book is Organized
    A Quick Note About Ever-Changing Technology
    Let's Talk About Mindset
    Keeping It Light
    Let's Get Started

Getting Started with Technology
    Understanding Your Digital Toolbox: Choosing the Right Device for You — 7
    Getting to Know Your Smartphone: The Ultimate Pocket-Sized Assistant — 12
    Mastering Your Tablet: The Ultimate Tool for Fun and Everyday Tasks — 18

Getting Started with Your Computer: Your New Digital Assistant	24
Making Technology Work for You: Exploring Accessibility Features	30

The Internet

Navigating the Internet: Your Guide to the World Wide Web	38
Mastering the Basics of Browsing: Your Guide to Exploring the Internet	43
Staying Safe Online: Your Digital Shield Against Scams and Sneaky Tricks	50

Digital Communication

Staying Connected: Your Guide to Easy, Modern Communication Tools	58
Getting Started with Email	63
The Art of Texting	69
Bringing Loved Ones Closer with Video Calls	76

Digital Photos

Mastering Digital Photography	86
Organizing Your Digital Memories	92
Sharing Your Special Moments	98

Staying Organized

- Handy Helpers — 106
- Your Digital Datebook — 111
- Remembering Made Easy — 117
- Time on Your Side — 123
- Your Handy Digital Notebook — 129

Social Media

- Staying Connected — 136
- Welcome to Facebook — 142
- Welcome to Instagram — 149
- Welcome to X (Formerly Twitter) — 156
- Entertainment

Reading News Online

- Your Guide to Staying Informed: Exploring News Websites and Apps with Ease — 182
- Staying Informed: How to Find Trustworthy News in a Digital World — 188

Smart Homes

- A Cozy Guide to Smart Homes: Making Life Easier, One Device at a Time — 195

Getting Started with Smart Speakers: Your Friendly Guide to Making Your Home Smarter	200

Shopping Online

Shopping from Home: A Beginner's Guide to Online Shopping	208
Starting with Online Shopping	214

Using Navigation Apps

Navigating the World with GPS	221
Using GPS	226

AI Tools

AI Demystified: Your Guide to Understanding and Using Artificial Intelligence	234
Making AI Your New Best Friend	238

Wrapping Up

Wrapping Up with Your Digital Grandson: A Friendly Tech Farewell	246
The Digital Grandson's Tech Glossary: Your Friendly Guide to Tech Terms	251
About The Digital Grandson's Guide to Tech	274

Welcome

A Friendly Guide to Starting Your Tech Journey

Have you ever asked someone for help with technology, only to find yourself staring at scribbled notes later, thinking, What on earth did I mean by this? **I get it.** And that's exactly why I'm here—to be your tech-savvy guide, walking you through everything step by step, like the digital grandson you didn't know you had.

Whether you're brand new to technology or just brushing up on your skills, let's take this journey together. My job is to help you feel comfortable, confident, and yes, even excited about the devices and tools around you. It's okay if things seem a little overwhelming right now—those buttons, screens, and endless notifications can feel like they're written in a secret code. But trust me, we'll decode it all. You've got this, and I'm here to help.

You're Not Alone

When you think about technology, you might feel a mix of curiosity and hesitation. Maybe you've watched others swipe effortlessly through their smartphones or type away on their laptops and wondered, How do they make it look so easy? Here's the good news: with a little guidance and practice, you can make it look just as easy.

Technology really is for everyone—yes, that includes you! It's never too late to learn. In fact, millions of people of all ages are learning about technology every day. Even your tech-savvy grandkids had to start somewhere. (I promise they didn't pop out of the womb knowing how to use TikTok!)

Of course, there will be moments when you feel frustrated. Maybe you'll tap the wrong button or forget where something is. That's completely normal. Just last week, I sent a text to the wrong person by accident—talk about awkward! It happens to all of us. The great thing about technology? There's always a way to fix it, and I'll show you how.

By the end of this book, you'll feel proud of how far you've come. Those intimidating devices? They'll start to feel like helpful companions. While this guide won't answer every single question, it'll give you a solid foundation to build on, so you'll always know what to ask next time you need a little help.

The Purpose of This Book

My goal is simple: to make technology accessible, enjoyable, and even fun.

We'll go step by step, using everyday language and simple comparisons to break down complicated ideas. Think of it this way: sending an email is like mailing a letter (but much faster!), and using Wi-Fi is like tuning into your favorite radio station. By tackling things one bite-sized piece at a time, you'll see that there's nothing here you can't handle.

How This Book is Organized

This book is designed with you in mind. You don't have to read it cover to cover (unless you want to!). If you're unpacking a brand-new laptop, there's a section for that. Want to set up an email address or stream Cheers on Netflix? Yep, I've got those covered too.

Feel free to skip around, revisit sections when you need a refresher, and go at your own pace. No one's watching to make sure you follow any particular order—if they are, kindly tell them to knock it off. I'll back you up!

And if you'd like even more resources, you can check out my website, **The Digital Grandson's Guide to Tech**. There, you'll find extra articles, videos, and even printable cheat sheets to keep handy. Have a question you don't see answered? Just send me a message—I'm here to help and always working to keep this guide up to date.

A Quick Note About Ever-Changing Technology

Technology evolves quickly. I've done my best to make sure everything here is current, but if you come across something that feels outdated or needs an update, let me know! Just visit **www.thedigitalgrandson.com** to send me a note. I'll look into it right away—together, we'll keep everything fresh.

Let's Talk About Mindset

Before we dive in, let's take a moment to talk about mindset. Learning something new—especially technology—can feel tricky at first. But if you approach it with curiosity and patience, you'll be amazed at what you can accomplish.

Think of it like learning to ride a bike. At first, it might feel awkward, and you might wobble a bit. But with a little practice, things start to click. The best part about learning tech? No scraped knees or bruises if you make a mistake! Press the wrong button? No big deal—there's almost always a way to reset or undo, and I'll show you how to handle those situations.

Actually, I encourage making mistakes. Every "oops" moment is an opportunity to learn something new. Sure, tech can be unforgiving sometimes—you press the wrong thing, and poof, it seems like everything disappears. But nothing is ever truly lost. Together, we'll find the way back, reset things, and keep going.

Keeping It Light

A sense of humor goes a long way when learning something new. Maybe you'll accidentally flip your screen upside down and feel like you're stuck in the Twilight Zone. Or maybe you'll send an email before it's ready—don't worry, we'll laugh it off together. I've made all these mistakes (and plenty more), and I promise they're all fixable.

So if something doesn't go right the first time, take a deep breath, have a chuckle, and remember: you're doing great.

Let's Get Started

By the end of this book, my hope is that you'll feel empowered, confident, and ready to explore all the amazing possibilities technology has to offer. Progress, not perfection, is the goal here. Every step forward, no matter how small, is a win.

So grab your device, get comfortable, and let's take this journey one step at a time. You're already off to a fantastic start just by being here. Let's do this together—I can't wait to see how far you'll go!

Getting Started with Technology

Digital Grandson Press

Understanding Your Digital Toolbox: Choosing the Right Device for You

Smartphones, Tablets, and Computers—Discover the Perfect Tools for Your Tech Journey

All right, let's get started with step one: understanding the different types of tech we'll be using. Think of your digital devices as tools in a toolbox. Just like you have specific tools for different tasks—like using a hammer to drive a nail or a whisk to beat eggs—each device has its own special purpose.

A smartphone, for example, is like a Swiss army knife: it can do almost anything. It's your camera, calculator, phone, and even a way to chat with family, all wrapped into one handy package. A tablet, on the other hand, is more like a trusty notebook—perfect for reading, jotting down notes, or watching your favorite show. Then there's the computer, which I like to think of as the workbench for all your devices. It's where the big jobs get done, whether that's organizing your photos or typing up a longer message.

The most important thing to remember is that every device is just a tool designed to help you. And, like with any household tool, there's a bit of a learning curve. Remember the first time you used a can opener? It might have felt a little confusing, but now you don't even think twice about it. It's the same with technology. With a bit of practice, these devices will start to feel as familiar as your favorite kitchen gadgets.

Don't Be Afraid to Explore

Here's a little secret: you're not going to break anything just by exploring! If you accidentally press the wrong button or end up on a screen you didn't expect, it's all part of the learning process. In fact, some of the best tech tricks I know, I learned by simply pressing buttons and seeing what happened. That's how you start making these devices feel like your own. I like to compare it to discovering a drawer in the kitchen that you hadn't opened in a while—sometimes you find something useful, and other times you find that random spatula you never use. Either way, you're learning where everything is!

A Quick Overview of Different Devices

Let's take a closer look at the devices you might be using:

Smartphones
These are the small devices we often carry in our pockets or purses. A smartphone is incredibly versatile—it lets you make phone calls, send text messages, snap photos, and even use maps to help you find your way. Think of it as your personal assistant, always ready to help you out. I remember the first time I figured out how to use the voice feature to send a text—it felt like magic! And yes, I may have accidentally told it to send a message that made no sense at all, but that's part of the fun.

Tablets

Next up are tablets. A tablet is a bit bigger than a smartphone but smaller than a computer. It's perfect for reading, watching movies, and playing games. Imagine a book that comes to life, where you can turn the pages with a simple swipe of your finger and have access to every story with the touch of a button. Tablets are great because they're big enough to see comfortably but still light enough to hold easily. I love using mine to look up new recipes while I'm cooking—it's like having a mini TV right on the counter!

Computers

Finally, we have computers, which can be either stationary desktops or portable laptops. A computer acts as your central hub for bigger tasks, like organizing your photo collection, typing up a longer email, or video chatting with family members. Computers might seem powerful (and they are!), but they don't have to be intimidating. Once you get the hang of it, a computer can feel like your very own command center, ready to help you tackle whatever you need. I remember the first time I joined a video call on my computer—I was so nervous I might press the wrong button and disconnect everyone. But now, it's one of my favorite ways to catch up with friends.

Choosing the Right Device for You

It's completely fine if you prefer one type of device over another. Maybe you enjoy using your smartphone but feel unsure about the computer—that's perfectly normal. If you're mostly interested in staying connected with family, a smartphone might be your best tool. If you love reading or watching shows, you might find a tablet more enjoyable. And if you like organizing photos or working on projects, a computer could be just the thing.

The key is figuring out what feels comfortable for you. And here's the best part: once you get comfortable with one device, you'll notice that the skills start to transfer to others. It's like learning how to use one tool in your shed—the more you practice, the easier it gets to learn the next one.

Celebrate Each Step Forward

The most important thing is to celebrate every little step you take. Maybe today you figured out how to turn on your tablet or adjust the volume on your smartphone—that's fantastic! Every small victory builds your confidence and brings you closer to mastering these tools. I'm right here with you, and I promise we'll take it one step at a time.

And if you ever get stuck, just take a deep breath, laugh it off, and keep trying. Even the best of us occasionally forget how to change the batteries in the remote control—I can't tell you how many times I've done that! The key is to keep a sense of humor and remember that you're doing great.

Let's Keep Going

Before you know it, you'll be using these devices like a pro. So let's keep moving forward together, exploring and learning as we go. And remember, I'm right here with you every step of the way.

And just to leave you with a smile: I still sometimes end up with the screen upside down when I'm trying to show someone a photo—it's a good reminder that we're all learning, no matter how experienced we are!

Getting to Know Your Smartphone: The Ultimate Pocket-Sized Assistant

Master the Basics of Your New Device—From Navigating Apps to Charging Like a Pro

What Is a Smartphone?

A smartphone is much more than just a phone—it's like carrying a small computer in your pocket. Sure, you can make phone calls, but you can also send messages, browse the internet, take photos, and even play games. Think of a smartphone as a hybrid of a traditional phone, a camera, and a pocket-sized assistant that helps you stay organized.

If you remember the days of rotary phones or those early cell phones that could only make calls, a smartphone might feel like a big leap forward. But don't worry—with a little practice, you'll have everything at your fingertips. You just tap on different icons (those little pictures on the screen) to open apps, which are programs that help you do all sorts of tasks.

> **Icon**: A small symbol or picture on your screen that represents an app, file, or command. Tapping an icon opens or activates that item.

> **App**: A software program you can download to your smartphone, tablet, or computer to perform specific tasks, like navigation, shopping, or communication.

Navigating Your Smartphone

Smartphones are designed to be intuitive, meaning they're made to be easy to use with just your fingers. You don't need a mouse or keyboard—just tap, swipe, or pinch the screen to get things done. Modern smartphones use capacitive touchscreens, which respond to the touch of your fingers, making them highly sensitive and easy to use.

Take a moment right now to find the power button on your phone and practice turning it on and off. Occasionally powering off your phone can also help resolve performance issues if it starts acting sluggish.

Think of your smartphone as a multi-purpose device for communication, entertainment, and organization. Unlike older phones that were mainly used for making calls, today's smartphones are versatile and capable of handling almost anything. It's your go-to device for sending messages, setting reminders, and much more.

A Quick Note on Safety

While exploring your phone, feel free to try tapping different icons and features—you won't break anything by looking around!

However, when you're downloading new apps or clicking on unfamiliar links, it's good to be cautious. Some apps may not come from trusted sources, especially on Android devices that may use alternative app stores like Huawei's AppGallery. If something seems unfamiliar or you're not sure about it, don't hesitate to ask for help or look it up first. It's all part of keeping your phone safe and secure.

Turning On Your Smartphone

Let's start with the basics: turning on your smartphone. While you don't often need to turn it off completely (most people just let it rest), it's good to know how to power it up.

- **Find the Power Button**: This is usually located on the side or top of your phone. Press and hold it for a few seconds until the screen lights up. Occasionally turning off your phone can help resolve issues like freezing apps or connectivity problems.

Navigating the Home Screen

The home screen is the first thing you see when you unlock your phone. Think of it as your control center, where you can access all your apps and settings.

- **Apps and Icons**: Your home screen is covered in icons, which look like small pictures representing different apps. It's like a workbench with all your tools laid out in front of you. Tap an icon, like the camera, to open that app.

- **Swiping Between Screens**: If you have a lot of apps, they may not all fit on one screen. Simply swipe left or right with your finger, just like turning a page in a book.

- **The Dock**: At the bottom of your home screen, you'll find a row of icons that stay in place as you swipe. This is called the dock, where you keep your favorite or most-used apps. It's like keeping your go-to tools at the front of your toolbox.

- **Notification Bar**: At the top of your screen is the notification bar, which shows important information like the time, battery level, and new messages. Swipe down from the top to see more details—it's like a bulletin board keeping you up to date.

- **Control Center**: On most iPhones, swipe down from the top-right corner to access quick settings. On older iPhones with a home button, swipe up from the bottom. For Android devices, swipe down from the top, but keep in mind that gestures can vary slightly depending on the phone model.

Accessibility Features

Most smartphones have accessibility options to help make them easier to use. You can adjust the text size to make it larger, use voice commands instead of tapping, or even enable features that read the screen out loud. If tapping feels tricky or the text is too small, try exploring these options—they're designed to make your phone work better for you.

Silencing Your Phone

There are times when you need your phone to be quiet, like during a movie or while you're sleeping. Here's how to do it:

- **Volume Buttons**: Press the down volume button until your phone vibrates or goes silent.

- **Do Not Disturb**: Enable this feature to silence all notifications and calls. You can usually find it by swiping down from the top of the screen.

- **Silent Switch (for iPhones)**: There's a small switch above the volume buttons—flip it to quickly silence your phone. For Android phones, use the volume buttons or enable "Do Not Disturb" mode.

Charging Your Phone

To keep your smartphone running, you'll need to charge it regularly.

- **Using a Charging Cable**: Plug the cable into your phone's charging port (usually at the bottom), then connect it to a power adapter and plug it into an outlet.

- **Wireless Charging**: If your phone supports it, place it on a wireless charging pad. Make sure your phone case isn't too thick, as this can interfere with charging.

- **Battery Tips**: To help extend your battery's lifespan, try to keep your phone's charge between 20% and 80% when possible.

Buttons and Ports

Your smartphone comes with a few basic buttons and ports that help you control it.

- **Volume Buttons**: These are on the side of your phone. One increases the volume (+), and the other decreases it (–), just like turning the knob on a radio.

- **Power Button**: This button not only turns your phone on and off but also puts it to sleep, which means the screen goes dark to save battery, but the phone stays on.

- **Ports**: At the bottom, you'll find the charging port, which is like a car's gas tank—it's where you refuel. While many newer phones don't include a headphone jack, some models still offer one, especially in mid-range or budget devices.

Take It One Step at a Time

Using a smartphone might feel overwhelming at first, especially if you're used to simpler devices. But remember, you don't need to learn everything at once. Start with the basics—calling, texting, or taking a photo. Each small step is a victory, and before you know it, you'll be swiping and tapping like a pro.

And just to leave you with a smile: I still sometimes open the wrong app when I'm in a hurry—it's a good reminder that we're all learning, no matter how much experience we have!

Mastering Your Tablet: The Ultimate Tool for Fun and Everyday Tasks

Discover How to Navigate, Customize, and Enjoy Your Tablet—One Tap at a Time

What Is a Tablet?

A tablet is like the perfect blend of a smartphone and a computer. Imagine if a computer and a phone had a baby—that's a tablet. It's flat, lightweight, and has a large touchscreen that makes it easy to use. Tablets are great for activities like reading, browsing the web, watching videos, and playing games.

Think of a tablet as a portable entertainment center and library all in one. It's light enough to carry around the house or take with you when you go out. With just a tap, you can easily switch from checking the news to watching a cooking video. It's like having a magical notebook that can do almost anything.

Tablets come in a variety of sizes, so you can choose one that suits your needs. Some are small and portable, while others have larger screens that are perfect for reading or watching videos. Whether you want something compact or a bigger screen for better viewing, there's a tablet that's right for you.

One of the best things about tablets is that they don't need much setup. You don't need a separate keyboard or mouse—just your fingers. This makes them feel more natural, especially if you're used to touching books or magazines. It feels less like "using technology" and more like interacting with something familiar.

Turning the Device On

Just like with your phone, you probably won't need to turn your tablet off very often. To turn it on, look for the power button. Depending on the model, it may be on the side, top edge, or near the rear camera. Hold it down for a few seconds until the screen lights up.

If your tablet feels slow or an app isn't responding, turning it off and back on can help. On some Samsung tablets, you might need to press and hold both the side button and the volume down button at the same time to access the power-off menu, as the side button may be configured to activate Bixby.

Navigating the Home Screen

The home screen is like the main control center of your tablet. When you turn it on, this is the first screen you'll see, filled with all your apps and settings.

- **Apps and Icons**: The home screen is covered with icons, which are small pictures that represent different apps. It's like looking at a bookshelf and deciding which book to read. Tap the camera icon to open the camera app, or tap the mail icon to check your emails.

- **Swiping Between Screens**: If you have a lot of apps, they might not all fit on one screen. Just swipe left or right with your finger, like turning the pages of a book, to see more apps.

- **The Dock**: At the bottom of the screen, there's a row of icons that stay in place even when you swipe between screens. This is called the dock. It's where you keep your favorite or most-used apps, like keeping your most-used tools at the front of your workbench.

- **Notification Bar**: At the top of the screen, you'll see the notification bar. It shows important information like the time, battery level, and new notifications. Swipe down from the top to see more details, like new messages or updates.

Accessing the Control Center

On many tablets, you can access quick settings through a control center. However, the gesture may vary depending on the device:

- **For iPads**: If you're using an iPad running iOS 12 or later, swipe down from the top-right corner of the screen to access the Control Center. On older iPads, swipe up from the bottom.

- **For Android Tablets**: Swipe down from the top of the screen to access quick settings, but note that the gesture may differ slightly based on the manufacturer.

Some iPads allow you to customize the Control Center, but this feature is only available on models running iOS 11 or later. If your iPad has an older version, this option may not be available.

If you want more tips on customizing your tablet's settings, check out The Digital Grandson's website for step-by-step guides. I've put together some easy tutorials to help you get the most out of your device.

Adjusting Volume, Buttons, and Ports

Knowing the basic buttons and ports on your tablet can help you use it more easily.

- **Volume Buttons**: These are usually on the side of your tablet. One button turns the volume up (+), and the other turns it down (–), just like adjusting the volume on an old radio. If you accidentally blast the sound, consider it a quick hearing test—you can always turn it back down!

- **Power Button**: The power button not only turns your device on and off but also puts it to sleep. If you tap the power button once, the screen turns off to save battery, but the tablet stays on, ready to wake up with another press. It's like putting a book down without losing your place.

- **Ports**: Most tablets have a charging port at the bottom where you plug in the charging cable. Some also have a headphone jack for wired headphones, which is perfect if you want to listen to music or watch a movie privately.

How Tablets Are Different From Computers and Phones

- **Tablets vs. Computers**: Compared to traditional computers, tablets are smaller, lighter, and more portable. While computers are great for big tasks like writing documents or managing lots of files, tablets are perfect for quick, casual use. I remember trying to use my tablet for a big project once and quickly missing the full keyboard. It's a good reminder that tablets are great for relaxing, but sometimes a computer is just easier for certain tasks.

- **Tablets vs. Phones**: Tablets are basically larger versions of smartphones. The bigger screen makes reading and watching videos much easier on the eyes. It's like watching a movie on a big TV instead of a small one—the larger screen just makes everything feel better! Plus, tablets often have better speakers, so the sound is richer and more enjoyable. Whether you're watching a show or listening to music, the experience feels a bit more special.

Tablets are perfect for activities where you need more space but don't want the hassle of a full computer setup. Whether you're looking at family photos, reading recipes while cooking, or video chatting with loved ones, a larger screen can make all the difference. And with a touchscreen, it's as simple as tapping, swiping, or pinching to zoom—just like you're holding something in your hands.

Take It One Step at a Time

Remember, there's no right or wrong way to use a tablet—it's all about what works best for you. Maybe today you'll read a new recipe, and tomorrow you'll video chat with a friend. Each time you use your tablet, you're building your confidence, which is worth celebrating.

And as I always say—progress over perfection! Let's keep learning and having fun along the way. You're not alone in this; I'm right here with you, cheering you on every step of the way.

No matter how long you've been using a tablet, there's always something new to discover—that's part of the fun! So take your time, enjoy exploring, and know that we're in this together, one tap at a time.

Getting Started with Your Computer: Your New Digital Assistant

Learn the Basics of Using Desktops and Laptops—Step by Step, with Your Digital Grandson by Your Side

What Is a Computer?

A computer is a versatile machine that can handle all sorts of tasks, from writing documents and browsing the internet to storing photos and staying in touch with loved ones. Think of it as an electronic assistant that helps with work, entertainment, and communication. There are two main types of computers: desktops, which are larger and stay in one place, and laptops, which are smaller and portable, making them easy to use anywhere.

A computer combines the functions of a typewriter, calculator, and filing cabinet. It lets you type letters, send emails, watch videos, and even play games. The screen, known as a monitor, displays everything you're doing, while the keyboard and mouse help you control it. It's like having a helpful assistant at your fingertips, ready to assist you with anything you need, whether it's finding a new recipe or catching up with friends.

Turning On Your Computer

Let's start with the basics: turning on your computer. It's easier than it looks! Every computer has a power button, usually marked with a symbol that looks like a circle with a line through it.

- **Desktop Computers**: Look for the power button on the front or side of the computer tower (the box-like part). Press it gently and wait for the screen to light up.

- **Laptops**: The power button is usually found above the keyboard, in the upper right or left corner. Just press it, and your laptop will wake up.

- **Mac vs. PC**:

    - **MacBook (2016 and later)**: The power button is integrated with the Touch ID sensor at the top-right corner of the keyboard, above the Delete key.

    - **Older MacBooks (2015 and earlier)**: The power button is a separate circular button located in the top-right corner of the keyboard.

    - **iMac**: The power button is located on the back of the monitor, in the lower right-hand corner when viewed from the front.

    - **Mac Mini**: The power button is on the back of the device, on the far-left side when viewed from the rear.

Be patient while your computer starts up—it's a bit like waiting for a pot of water to boil. It may take a few moments, but soon it will be ready for you to use. And if you're like me, it's the perfect time to grab a quick cup of coffee.

Understanding the Desktop Screen

Once your computer starts up, you'll see the desktop screen. Think of it as your digital desk where you can find everything you need. You'll see small pictures called icons, which represent different programs or files. For example, an icon that looks like a piece of paper might represent a document, while a small blue "e" could be your internet browser.

- **Mac vs. PC**: On a Windows PC, you'll often find the Start menu in the bottom-left corner, which gives you access to programs and settings. On a Mac, instead of a Start menu, there's a Dock at the bottom of the screen with icons for your favorite programs. The menu bar at the top of the screen contains important options and settings.

Adjusting Volume, Buttons, and Ports

Understanding your computer's basic buttons and ports will make using it much easier.

- **Volume Control**: Most computers have volume buttons on the keyboard, usually marked with speaker icons. You can also adjust the volume by clicking the volume icon on the screen. On a PC, this icon is in the bottom-right corner, while on a Mac, it's in the top-right. Don't worry if you accidentally blast the sound—it's a good way to check if your hearing is still sharp!

- **USB Ports**: These are rectangular slots where you can plug in accessories like a mouse, keyboard, or USB drive. Think of USB ports as universal connectors—they let you attach a variety of devices.

- **Headphone Jack**: Some computers have a small round port for headphones, usually on the side of a laptop or the front of a desktop. It's perfect for private listening, like plugging headphones into an old stereo.

- **Power Button**: The power button also puts the computer to sleep, saving energy while keeping everything ready when you return. Just a quick tap puts it to sleep, but try not to hold it down to turn off the computer—that's only for emergencies. Instead, use the proper shutdown process.

Shutting Down Your Computer

Shutting down your computer properly helps it run smoothly and keeps your files safe.

- **Windows PC**: Click the Start menu, then select the Power icon and choose Shut Down. Make sure to save any open documents first.

- **Mac**:
    - Click the Apple logo in the top-left corner of your screen and select "Shut Down."
    - You can also use the keyboard shortcut **Control + Option + Command + Power button** to shut down immediately.

- If your Mac becomes unresponsive, you can force a shutdown by holding the power button for about 5 seconds. However, this should only be done as a last resort to avoid losing unsaved data.

If you're unsure about any of these steps, head over to The Digital Grandson's website for quick video tutorials and extra help. I've put together simple guides to walk you through it.

Using the Mouse, Trackpad, and Keyboard

Once your computer is on, you'll use two main tools: the mouse (or trackpad) and the keyboard.

- **Mouse**: The mouse is like your hand on the screen. Move it around, and you'll see a small arrow (the pointer) move with it. Click the mouse button to select things, and double-click to open programs. It's like pointing at what you want and then pressing a button to choose it.

- **Trackpad**: If you're using a laptop, you may use a trackpad instead of a mouse. The trackpad is a touch-sensitive surface under the keyboard. Move your finger on the trackpad to control the pointer, and tap it to click. On a Mac, you can use multi-finger gestures like scrolling (two fingers) or zooming (pinch with two fingers). It might take a bit of practice, but once you get the hang of it, you'll feel like a pro!

- **Keyboard**: The keyboard is for typing letters, numbers, and symbols. It's similar to a typewriter but with more options. Start with the basics, like typing your name or a short note. If you make a mistake, just press the Backspace (or Delete on a Mac) key to erase it.

Take It One Step at a Time

Using a computer might feel intimidating at first, but remember, it's all about taking it step by step. Today, you might learn how to turn it on and use the mouse. Tomorrow, you might open your first program or type a quick message. Each small step is a victory, and before you know it, these basics will become second nature.

Did you open an application or type your name today? That's fantastic! Every small success is a step forward. Even tech experts had to start from the beginning. So if you ever get frustrated, take a deep breath, smile, and remember—progress over perfection. You're doing great, and I'm right here with you every step of the way.

Making Technology Work for You: Exploring Accessibility Features

Discover Simple Tools to Personalize Your Device and Enhance Your Experience—With a Little Help From Your Digital Grandson

Overview of Useful Accessibility Features

Technology can feel tricky at times, but smartphones, tablets, and computers come with a lot of built-in features designed to make things easier. These are called "accessibility features," and they're like helpful tools that adapt your device to meet your needs, rather than the other way around. Whether it's making text larger, using voice commands, or magnifying part of the screen, these features can make a big difference in your tech experience.

Let's go through some of the most useful accessibility features you can try. Remember, we're figuring this out together—it's all about finding what works best for you!

Text Size Adjustment

If the text on your device feels too small, you can make it bigger—like using a digital magnifying glass, but without the hassle. Adjusting the text size can make reading messages, articles, or menus much more comfortable and help reduce eye strain.

How to Change Text Size on a Smartphone or Tablet:

- **iPhone or iPad**: Open the Settings app and tap on "Display & Brightness." Then select "Text Size" and use the slider to increase or decrease the size. You can also go to "Accessibility" > "Display & Text Size" for additional options like Bold Text.

- **Android**: Open the Settings app, then tap "Display" followed by "Font Size." Use the slider to make the text bigger or smaller. You can also find more options under "Accessibility" > "Text and Display."

How to Change Text Size on a Computer:

- **Windows PC**: Click the Start menu, then select "Settings." Go to "Ease of Access," and choose "Display." Use the slider under "Make text bigger" to adjust the size.

- **Mac**: Click the Apple menu, then select "System Settings." Choose "Displays," and adjust the text size or resolution. For more options, go to "Accessibility" > "Display."

Voice Commands

Voice commands let you control your device without lifting a finger. It's like having a little helper who's always ready to listen and follow your instructions. Instead of typing or tapping, you can simply say what you need, like "Call John" or "Set a reminder for 2 PM." I remember showing my grandmother how to use Siri for the first time—she asked, "Siri, are you single?" We had a good laugh, and it was a great way to break the ice!

How to Use Voice Commands on a Smartphone or Tablet:

- **iPhone or iPad**: Say "Hey Siri" to give a command, or hold down the side button (Touch ID button) to activate Siri. You'll see the Siri icon appear, letting you know it's ready to listen.

- **Android**: Say "Hey Google" to start speaking to Google Assistant. You can also activate it by pressing and holding the home button.

How to Use Voice Commands on a Computer:

- **Windows PC**: Click the Start menu and search for "Cortana," then click the icon to start using it. You can also press **Windows + C** to activate Cortana.

- **Mac**: Click the Siri icon in the menu bar or say "Hey Siri" if it's enabled in your System Preferences.

Magnifier Tool

When you need a closer look, the magnifier tool acts like a digital magnifying glass. It's great for zooming in on small text or images, making it easier to see the details. If you're ever unsure about using this tool, don't worry—we'll figure it out together.

How to Enable the Magnifier Tool:

- **iPhone or iPad**: Go to "Settings" > "Accessibility" and tap "Magnifier" to turn it on. You can now access it quickly by triple-clicking the side button.

- **Android**: Open "Settings" > "Accessibility," then tap "Magnification." You can turn it on and choose whether to use a shortcut or a gesture to activate it.

- **Windows PC**: Press **Windows + Plus (+)** to open the Magnifier tool. To close it, press **Windows + Escape**.

- **Mac**: Click the Apple menu, then select "System Settings" > "Accessibility." Choose "Zoom" to enable the magnifier options.

Screen Reader

A screen reader reads aloud the text on your screen, like having someone read you a book. It's a great feature if your eyes are tired or you prefer listening over reading. Trying out a screen reader for the first time can feel like discovering a hidden superpower!

How to Enable a Screen Reader:

- **iPhone or iPad**: Go to "Settings" > "Accessibility" and tap

"VoiceOver" to enable it.

- **Android**: Go to "Settings" > "Accessibility" and tap "TalkBack" to turn it on.

- **Windows PC**: Press **Windows + Ctrl + Enter** to activate Narrator.

- **Mac**: Click the Apple menu, then go to "System Settings" > "Accessibility" and select "VoiceOver."

High Contrast Mode

High Contrast Mode changes the colors on your screen to make text stand out more clearly. It's like putting on a pair of glasses that make everything pop—suddenly, the fine print isn't so 'fine' anymore!

How to Enable High Contrast Mode:

- **iPhone or iPad**: Go to "Settings" > "Accessibility," then tap "Display & Text Size" and enable "Increase Contrast."

- **Android**: Open "Settings" > "Accessibility" and tap "High Contrast Text."

- **Windows PC**: Go to "Settings" > "Ease of Access," then select "High Contrast."

- **Mac**: Click the Apple menu, then go to "System Settings" > "Accessibility" and select "Display."

Assistive Touch

Assistive Touch adds a floating button to your screen, making it easier to access certain features without using physical buttons. It's like having an extra pair of hands on your device.

How to Use Assistive Touch:

- **iPhone or iPad**: Go to "Settings" > "Accessibility," then tap "Touch" and select "AssistiveTouch."

- **Android**: Open "Settings" > "Accessibility," then select "Accessibility Menu."

- **Windows PC**: Search for "On-Screen Keyboard" in the Start menu.

- **Mac**: Go to "System Settings" > "Accessibility" and choose "Keyboard."

Closed Captions

Closed captions display the text of what's being said in a video. It's like reading along while someone speaks, helping you catch every word even if there's background noise.

How to Enable Closed Captions:

- **iPhone or iPad**: Go to "Settings" > "Accessibility" > "Subtitles & Captioning."

- **Android**: Open "Settings" > "Accessibility" > "Caption Preferences."

- **Windows PC**: Go to "Settings" > "Ease of Access" > "Closed Captions."

- **Mac**: Click the Apple menu, then go to "System Settings" > "Accessibility" and select "Captions."

Take It One Step at a Time

These features are here to make your device work better for you. Don't be afraid to experiment and try different settings. Every small victory is worth celebrating, and you're taking control of your technology one tap at a time.

And remember, progress over perfection—we're learning together, one step at a time. You've got this!

The Internet

DIGITAL GRANDSON PRESS

Navigating the Internet: Your Guide to the World Wide Web

Learn How to Connect, Browse, and Discover—With Your Digital Grandson Leading the Way

Welcome to the Wonderful World of the Internet!

Now, before you sigh and think, "This is where it all gets confusing," take a deep breath—I promise we'll go through it step by step. The internet, like learning to ride a bike or making your first cup of coffee, might seem tricky at first, but it's also full of surprises, fun, and endless useful information. Even if you're thinking, "I don't even know what the internet is," you're in the right place. We're exploring this together, and I promise it's not as complicated as it seems!

What Is the Internet?

Think of the internet as a giant library, but instead of shelves filled with books, it's packed with websites, photos, videos, and more information than you could ever imagine. Remember those old switchboard operators who plugged wires to connect phone calls? The internet works a bit like that, but on a much larger scale—it's a giant digital switchboard connecting people, information, and devices all over the world. And here's the best part: you don't need to connect any wires yourself. All you need is a device that can connect to the internet, and I'm right here to guide you!

Let's break it down simply:

- The internet is a network that links millions of computers worldwide.

- It lets us read the news, make video calls with family, send emails, and even watch funny cat videos (trust me, there are plenty of those out there!).

- You can look up information, shop for new items, and even learn new skills—just like you're doing right now!

Why Use the Internet?

You might be wondering, "Why would I want to use this internet thing anyway?" Great question! Here are some ways the internet can be useful for you:

- **Staying in Touch**: Do you remember when letters were the main way to communicate? Now, the internet gives us email and video calls, so you can send messages instantly or even see the smiling faces of your loved ones, no matter where they are. I remember helping my grandparents set up their first video call—they couldn't believe they could see my face from miles away. It was like magic!

- **Learning New Things**: It's like having an entire encyclopedia at your fingertips. Whether you want to learn about gardening, try a new recipe, or discover tips for a home project, everything you need is just a few clicks away.

- **Entertainment**: There's something for everyone—movies, music, books, and even funny videos of people stepping on their kids' toys (we've all been there!). The internet is a great place to relax and have fun.

Getting Connected: What You Need to Know

Now that you know what the internet is, let's talk about how to get connected. Here are a few terms you might hear:

- **Wi-Fi**: This is like an invisible cord that connects your device to the internet. Think of it as tuning into a radio station—your device "tunes in" to the internet through Wi-Fi, and you're connected. I remember setting up Wi-Fi for my grandparents for the first time. My grandpa joked, "So, the internet is just floating around our living room now?" It was a good laugh and a fun way to explain it!

- **Router**: This is the little box that broadcasts the Wi-Fi signal throughout your home. It's like the DJ at a party, playing music for everyone to hear. Instead of music, it sends out the internet signal that your devices use.

The good news is, you usually don't have to set up the router yourself—that's typically done by your internet provider. You might need to turn it off and back on once in a while if something isn't working, but don't worry—we'll go through that together when it happens.

The Magic of Browsing

Once you're connected to the internet, the fun really begins—this is where browsing comes in. Browsing just means exploring the internet and searching for things you're interested in. It's a bit like wandering through a shopping mall, but instead of stores, you're visiting different websites.

- **Web Browser**: To browse the internet, you need a web browser. Think of it as your car—it's what gets you around the internet. Some popular browsers are Google Chrome, Firefox, Microsoft Edge, and Safari. If you're not sure which one to use, head over to The Digital Grandson's website for a quick video guide on choosing a browser.

- **Web Address**: Just like your home has an address, each website has its own address too, called a web address or URL. These usually start with "www" and end with ".com," ".org," or something similar. To visit a website, you simply type its address into your browser.

Browsing the internet is like going on a little adventure—you never know what you'll find! It could be a recipe for the best apple pie or a video of a dog dressed as a superhero (trust me, it's out there!).

Final Thoughts

The fact that you're reading this right now is already a big win! You've taken the first step toward understanding the internet, and that's worth celebrating. Every time you learn something new, like what Wi-Fi is or how to use a web browser, it's another victory. And remember, it's perfectly okay if it takes a little time for everything to sink in—you're doing fantastic, and every small step counts.

If you ever feel stuck or unsure, visit The Digital Grandson's website. I've put together some easy tutorials and guides to help you out. We're always adding new resources to make your tech journey smoother.

And as I always say, progress over perfection. We're learning together, one click at a time. You've got this!

MASTERING THE BASICS OF BROWSING: YOUR GUIDE TO EXPLORING THE INTERNET

LEARN HOW TO NAVIGATE, SEARCH, AND SAVE YOUR FAVORITE SITES—WITH YOUR DIGITAL GRANDSON BY YOUR SIDE

Welcome to the World of Internet Browsing!

This chapter is all about helping you feel comfortable and confident when using the internet. Think of it as starting a new adventure—but instead of packing a suitcase, all you need are a few new skills and a sense of curiosity. The internet is a vast resource full of information, entertainment, and ways to connect with others. Let's take it one step at a time, and before you know it, you'll be browsing like a pro!

What Is a Web Browser?

A web browser is the tool you use to explore the internet. It's like your car—it helps you travel from one website to another. Some of the most popular web browsers are Google Chrome, Safari, Microsoft Edge, and Firefox. Each one does the same job, just with a slightly different look and feel.

Think about how you'd drive to the library to borrow a book. With a web browser, you can now access millions of books, articles, and videos right from your living room. (And the best part? No late fees!)

How to Open a Web Browser

Let's do this together:

- **On a Computer**: Look for a browser icon on your desktop or taskbar, like a colorful circle for Google Chrome or a blue "e" for Microsoft Edge. Just click on it, and you're ready to go.

- **On a Tablet or Smartphone**: Find an app that says "Internet" or has the name of your browser (like Safari or Chrome). Tap it to get started.

What Is a Website?

A website is like a digital version of a store, library, or newspaper. It's a place on the internet where information is gathered and shared. Each website has its own unique address, known as a URL, which helps you find it—just like a house address.

Most web addresses start with "www" and end with ".com," ".org," or something similar. For example, typing in **www.bbc.com** or **www.cnn.com** will take you straight to a news website.

How to Visit a Website

At the top of your web browser, you'll see a white box called the address bar. It's like the navigation system in your car—you type in where you want to go, and the browser takes you there.

For example, if you want to visit a news site, type **www.bbc.com** and press the Enter (or Return) key on your keyboard. The browser will take you directly to the website.

Search Engines: Your Online Library Assistant

A search engine is a tool that helps you find exactly what you're looking for on the internet. The most popular search engine is Google, but others include Bing and Yahoo. Think of a search engine like a helpful librarian. Instead of flipping through a card catalog, you simply type in what you're searching for, and the search engine finds it for you.

How to Use a Search Engine:

1. Open your web browser.

2. Type **www.google.com** into the address bar and press Enter.

3. You'll see a search box. Enter what you're curious about (like "easy dinner recipes" or "weather tomorrow") and press Enter.

4. Google will show a list of links to websites with the information you're looking for. Click on the one that looks most helpful.

If you'd like more tips on using Google or finding specific information online, check out The Digital Grandson's website. I've put together some easy video guides to help you out.

A Few Search Tips

- **Be Specific**: The more specific you are, the better your results will be. Instead of typing "flowers," try "how to care for tulips."

- **Use Simple Words**: There's no need for fancy language—just type what's on your mind. If you're curious, phrase it as a question, like "What's the best way to bake bread?"

- **Avoid Clicking Ads**: The first few links might be ads. These usually have the word "Ad" next to them. Scroll down a bit to find the regular results.

Tabs: Multitasking Made Easy

One of the great things about browsing the internet is that you can open multiple tabs—like having several books open at the same time. Each tab represents a different website, so you can easily switch between them.

How to Open a New Tab:
Look for a small "+" sign at the top of your browser window. Click it to open a new tab, then type a new address or search for something without leaving the page you were on. It's like having multiple windows open, but without the draft!

Bookmarks: Save Your Favorite Spots

Have you ever found a great website but couldn't remember how to get back to it later? That's where bookmarks come in handy. Bookmarks are like sticky notes that save the page for you, so you can easily return whenever you want.

How to Bookmark a Website:

1. When you find a website you like, click the star icon or the word "Bookmark" at the top of your browser.

2. To access your saved bookmarks, look in your browser's menu for a section called "Bookmarks" or "Favorites."

You just saved your first bookmark—how cool is that? It's a big deal because now you have a quick way back to your favorite spots online. High five for that win!

Using the Back, Forward, and Refresh Buttons

Browsing the internet can feel like flipping through a magazine. Sometimes, you'll want to go back to a page you just saw or refresh a page to see new updates.

- **Back Button**: This button looks like a left-facing arrow in the upper left corner of your browser. Click it to go back to the previous page.

- **Forward Button**: This right-facing arrow moves you forward again if you've gone back a page.

- **Refresh Button**: This button looks like a circular arrow. Click it if a page isn't loading properly or if you want to see updated information.

These buttons work like the navigation tools in your car, helping you stay in control of where you're going.

Remember to Be Safe While Browsing

Browsing the internet is fun, but it's important to stay safe. Here are a few tips:

- **Stick to Trusted Websites**: If you're unsure about a website, it's best to avoid it. Trusted sites like **BBC.com** and **NationalGeographic.com** are safe to use.

- **Avoid Clicking on Pop-Up Ads**: If you see ads that pop up, especially if they sound too good to be true, it's best to ignore them.

- **Look for "https"**: When entering personal information, make sure the web address starts with "https" and has a padlock icon. This means the site is secure.

Final Thoughts

Let's celebrate your progress! If you've made it this far, you've learned:

- How to open a web browser.

- What a website is and how to visit one.

- How to use Google to find information.

- How to open multiple tabs for multitasking.

- How to save your favorite websites with bookmarks.

These are big steps, and you should be proud of yourself. Learning something new can be challenging, but each click is a step forward. And as I always say, progress over perfection. We're learning together, one click at a time. You're doing amazing!

STAYING SAFE ONLINE: YOUR DIGITAL SHIELD AGAINST SCAMS AND SNEAKY TRICKS

LEARN HOW TO PROTECT YOURSELF AND NAVIGATE THE INTERNET WITH CONFIDENCE—WITH A LITTLE HELP FROM YOUR DIGITAL GRANDSON

Staying Safe Online: Your Guide to Navigating the Internet with Confidence

Welcome to a new and important phase of our digital journey: staying safe online. The internet is a wonderful place full of information, connections, and entertainment, but just like in the real world, there are a few things to watch out for. Imagine walking through a bustling marketplace—there are plenty of friendly faces, but it's wise to keep an eye on your wallet and know who to trust. Let's go over some simple steps to help you stay safe and confident while enjoying everything the internet has to offer. We're in this together!

Understanding Online Scams and Phishing

The internet can sometimes feel like the Wild West—mostly exciting, but with a few tricksters lurking around. Online scams and phishing attempts are like the old-fashioned con artists you see in movies, trying to trick people into giving away their money or personal information.

- **Online Scams**: These are sneaky schemes designed to get your money or personal details. They might show up as unbelievable deals (which are usually too good to be true). If you get a message saying you've won the lottery but never bought a ticket, it's almost certainly a scam.

- **Phishing**: This is like fishing, but with a twist—instead of catching fish, scammers try to "catch" people by tricking them into clicking fake links or sharing personal information. I remember the first time I saw a phishing email that looked like it was from my bank. It even used the same logo! Luckily, I trusted my gut and called the bank directly. It turns out it was a scam—my grandma always said, "If it feels fishy, it probably is!"

How to Spot a Scam or Phishing Attempt

1. **If It Sounds Too Good to Be True, It Probably Is**: Be cautious of messages offering large sums of money or extravagant prizes.

2. **Urgent Language**: Scammers often use words like "urgent" or "immediate action required" to make you feel pressured. Take a moment to pause and think before clicking.

3. **Strange Email Addresses**: If you receive an email from an odd address (like "bank12345@weirdsite.com"), it's likely a

scam.

4. **Unusual Requests**: Be wary if someone asks for sensitive information, like your credit card number or Social Security number.

If you're ever unsure about an email, don't hesitate to visit The Digital Grandson's website. I've added a quick guide on common email scams and how to handle them—let's stay one step ahead together.

What to Do If You Suspect a Scam

- **Don't Click on Links**: If you think an email or message is a scam, avoid clicking any links. It's better to be safe than sorry.

- **Contact the Real Source**: If you receive a suspicious message from your bank, call them using a trusted phone number, not the one provided in the message.

- **Report It**: Most email providers have a "Report Phishing" button. You can also report scams to the Federal Trade Commission (FTC) or your local authorities.

And remember, it's normal to feel nervous about this. Even the best of us have almost clicked on something suspicious before catching it just in time. Trust your instincts and double-check when in doubt.

Creating Strong Passwords and Using Password Managers

Let's talk about passwords—they're the keys to your digital home. Just like you wouldn't want an easy-to-copy key for your front door, your passwords should be strong and secure.

Tips for Creating Strong Passwords:

- **Make It Long**: Aim for at least twelve characters.

- **Mix It Up**: Use a combination of uppercase and lowercase letters, numbers, and symbols. It's like adding multiple locks to your door.

- **Avoid the Obvious**: Stay away from simple choices like "123456" or "password," and don't use personal information like your birthday or pet's name.

If you're thinking, "How am I supposed to remember all these complicated passwords?" don't worry—that's what a password manager is for!

- **Password Managers**: These are like a secure little black book for your passwords. They remember all your passwords, so you only have to remember one main password. It's like having a master key that unlocks everything you need. Your phone, tablet, or computer likely has a built-in password manager that can help you keep track.

Recognizing Suspicious Emails and Websites

You know how you can tell when a salesperson is being pushy, and something feels off? It's the same with emails and websites—sometimes your gut tells you something isn't right. Let's look at a few red flags.

Suspicious Emails

1. **Unfamiliar Senders**: Be cautious if you get an email from someone you don't know, especially if they're asking for personal information.

2. **Spelling and Grammar Mistakes**: Scam emails often have strange grammar or poor spelling. Legitimate companies usually send well-written messages.

3. **Unexpected Attachments**: If you receive an unexpected attachment, don't open it. It's like getting a mystery package from a stranger—better to leave it alone until you know it's safe.

4. **Requests for Personal Information**: No trustworthy company will ask you to share your password or sensitive information through email.

Suspicious Websites

1. **Look for "https"**: Check that the web address starts with "https"—the "s" stands for secure. Also, look for a small padlock icon in the address bar.

2. **Strange Pop-Ups and Ads**: If a website starts throwing pop-ups like confetti, it's time to leave the party! Legitimate sites rarely have excessive pop-ups.

3. **Check the URL**: Scammers sometimes create fake websites that look almost identical to real ones. Double-check the web address for small changes (like "amaz0n.com" instead of "amazon.com").

What to Do If You Visit a Suspicious Website

1. **Don't Panic**: Staying calm is rule #1.

2. **Close the Page**: If something feels off, simply close the browser window.

3. **Run a Security Scan**: If you think you might have clicked on something suspicious, use your antivirus software to perform a scan.

Final Thoughts

You've just learned how to spot a scam, create strong passwords, and navigate the internet safely—that's huge! You're already ahead of so many people out there. Let's take a moment to give yourself a well-deserved pat on the back. This is progress worth celebrating!

And as always, remember—progress over perfection. We're taking it one click at a time, and you're doing an amazing job. I'm proud of you for making it this far. Keep going—you've got this!

DIGITAL COMMUNICATION

DIGITAL GRANDSON PRESS

Staying Connected: Your Guide to Easy, Modern Communication Tools

Master Email, Texting, and Video Calls—With Your Digital Grandson as Your Guide

Connecting with Loved Ones: A Guide to Modern Communication Tools

Welcome to the wonderful world of communication tools! Staying in touch has never been easier, thanks to technology. Whether you want to call a loved one, send a quick message, or even see their smiling face on a video call, there's a tool for that. Don't worry—we'll take this one step at a time, and I'm right here beside you as we explore all the options together.

The Basics: What Are Communication Tools?

Think back to the days of rotary phones, handwritten letters, and even tin cans connected by string. Those were the ways we kept in touch back then. Today's communication tools are like high-tech versions of those old favorites. They help us talk, send messages, and stay close to the people we care about—no matter where they are.

Here are some of the most common communication tools you might hear about:

- **Email**: This stands for "electronic mail." It's like sending a letter, but instead of using an envelope and a stamp, you type your message on your device, and it gets delivered instantly to the recipient's inbox. Emails are perfect for longer messages or sharing news. They're the digital equivalent of the letters we used to send across long distances.

- **Text Messaging**: Text messages are quick, short messages you send from your phone. Imagine it like passing a note to someone, but it arrives instantly. Texting is great for quick updates, asking a question, or just saying, "I'm thinking of you." It's like sending a postcard, but without the stamps or the wait!

- **Video Calls**: Remember when it seemed futuristic to talk to someone on a screen? Well, that future is here, and we can do it every day with apps like Zoom, Skype, and FaceTime. I remember the first time I showed my grandparents how to use FaceTime. We ended up spending 10 minutes just laughing because they kept accidentally holding the phone up to their ear during the video call. It was a fun moment—and a great reminder that it's okay to make mistakes while learning!

- **Voice Calls Over the Internet**: This is like a regular phone call, but instead of using a phone line, it uses the internet. Apps like WhatsApp and Skype let you make voice calls for free, as long as you're connected to the internet. It's like making a call on a landline, but without worrying about long-distance charges.

- **Instant Messaging Apps**: Apps like WhatsApp, Facebook Messenger, and iMessage allow you to send messages instantly. They combine the features of text messaging and email, letting you send not just text but also photos, videos, and voice recordings. It's like sending a text message on steroids—you can share photos, videos, and even a voice recording of your grandkids saying "Hi!"

- **Social Media Messaging**: Many social media platforms, like Facebook and Instagram, have built-in messaging features. It's like mailing someone a note, but now you can share pictures, chat in real time, and keep up with everyone's updates—all in one place.

Choosing the Right Tool for the Job

Each of these tools has its own strengths, and choosing the right one depends on what you want to do:

- **Sharing Big News**: Use email for writing longer messages, sharing stories, and sending updates.

- **Need a Quick Answer?**: Send a text message or instant message. It's perfect for a quick question or a friendly hello.

- **Missing Someone?**: Make a video call to see and hear your loved one. There's something so special about being able to see a loved one's face light up, even if they're miles away. It's like turning back the clock to those heartwarming moments when you'd see a smile from across the room.

- **Just Want to Chat?**: A voice call is a great way to hear someone's voice without needing to type.

Don't worry if you're not sure which tool to use at first. We'll figure it out together, and soon enough, you'll know exactly when to send a quick text or hop on a video call. It's all about trying things out and seeing what works best for you.

Popular Apps to Help You Stay Connected

Let's look at a few popular apps (short for applications) that can help you stay in touch:

- **WhatsApp**: This is a versatile app that lets you send text messages, make voice calls, and have video chats—all for free as long as you're connected to the internet. It's like having a Swiss Army knife for communication!

- **Facebook Messenger**: If you use Facebook, Messenger is an easy way to chat with friends and family. It's integrated with your Facebook account, so it's simple to use and great for sharing updates.

- **Zoom**: Perfect for video calls, whether it's a one-on-one conversation or a virtual family gathering. It's like having a face-to-face chat without leaving the comfort of your home.

- **FaceTime**: If you have an Apple device, FaceTime is a great way to make video or voice calls with other Apple users. It's quick, easy, and built right into your device.

- **Skype**: Skype has been around for a long time and is still popular for both voice and video calls. It works on almost any device and is a reliable way to stay in touch, especially with loved ones who live far away.

If you'd like a step-by-step guide on setting up any of these apps, head over to The Digital Grandson's website. I've created easy-to-follow video tutorials to walk you through each one—we're here to help, every step of the way.

Final Thoughts

Modern communication tools have brought us closer together in ways we couldn't have imagined just a few decades ago. You don't have to wait weeks at the mailbox for a letter anymore—you can send a quick text, make a call, or see a loved one's face in moments.

It's completely normal to feel a bit unsure at first. You might worry about pressing the wrong button or not knowing which app to use. That's okay! Every tech expert out there was once a beginner, just like you. The key is to be curious and have a little fun while learning.

You've just learned about emails, texts, video calls, and messaging apps—that's a lot to take in, and you're doing an amazing job! Let's take a moment to give yourself a well-deserved pat on the back. This is progress worth celebrating!

And as always, remember—progress over perfection. We're learning together, one message at a time. You're doing an amazing job, and I'm so proud of how far you've come. Keep going—you've got this!

Getting Started with Email

Setting Up an Email Account with Confidence and Ease

Welcome to Your New Email Adventure!

Congratulations on taking the next step in your tech journey: setting up your very own email account!

Think of your email address as your own digital mailbox. It's where you can receive letters, updates, and newsletters from friends, family, and your favorite organizations. In this chapter, we'll walk through the basics of creating an email account, step by step. Don't worry—we'll go nice and slow, and I'll be here to guide you the whole way through.

What Is an Email Address?

Your email account is like a virtual post office box, a place to send and receive electronic messages. It's your unique online address, just like your home address directs physical mail to your doorstep. Your email address will look something like "yourname@example.com," and it helps people know where to send their digital letters.

With your own email address, you can easily:

- **Stay in Touch:** Share updates, photos, or just say a quick hello to friends and family, no matter where they are in the world.

- **Receive Important Updates:** Many businesses use email for bills, notifications, and reminders. It's a simple way to keep track of important information without relying on paper mail.

- **Sign Up for Things:** Want to join a website, shop online, or receive updates from your favorite club or store? An email address is your ticket in.

Having an email address is like opening a new door to endless possibilities—from reconnecting with old friends to discovering new hobbies. It's a digital bridge that helps you stay connected to the world around you.

Choosing an Email Provider

Before you can set up an email account, you'll need to choose an email provider. Think of this step like picking a post office where you want to set up your mailbox. There are a few popular options, and they all offer similar services. Here's a quick look at the most common ones:

- **Gmail:** Google's email service is easy to use and works well on computers, tablets, and smartphones. Plus, it connects seamlessly with other Google services like Google Drive and Google Photos.

- **Yahoo Mail:** Known for its user-friendly design and plenty of storage space, Yahoo Mail is a good choice if you're already familiar with it.

- **Outlook:** This service from Microsoft is great if you use tools like Word or Excel. Outlook also includes a built-in calendar, making it handy for keeping track of appointments.

- **iCloud Mail:** If you have an Apple device like an iPhone or iPad, iCloud Mail might be the easiest choice. It works well with other Apple apps, making it a natural fit for Apple users.

All of these providers offer free email services, so it's just a matter of picking one that feels right for you.

Setting Up Your Email Account

Setting up your email account is like putting up a brand-new mailbox—it's where your messages will be delivered, and it's easy to do. Let's go through it step by step.

1. **Choose a Provider:** Start by picking which email service you'd like to use. For this guide, we'll use Gmail as an example, but the process is similar for other providers.

2. **Go to the Website:** Open your web browser (like Chrome, Safari, or Edge) and type in the website address, such as "www.gmail.com."

3. **Create an Account:** Look for a button that says "Create account" or "Sign up." Click on it to begin.

4. **Enter Your Information:** You'll need to provide some basic details like your name, birthday, and your preferred email address. If your first choice isn't available, don't worry! You might need to get creative by adding a middle initial or some numbers (e.g., "John.E.Smith@gmail.com").

5. **Create a Password:** Your password is the key to your mailbox, so make it strong. Use a mix of letters, numbers, and symbols. Instead of something obvious like "123456," try using a memorable phrase like "MyDogLovesBones123!"

6. **Enable Two-Factor Authentication (2FA):** If you see an option for two-factor authentication, consider enabling it. This extra step will help protect your account by sending a code to your phone whenever you log in from a new device.

7. **Verify Your Information:** You might be asked to confirm your identity by entering a code sent to your phone. This helps keep your account secure.

8. **Start Using Your Email:** You did it! You now have your very own email address. You can start sending messages and receiving updates right away.

Understanding Your Inbox

Your inbox is like the mail slot in your home—it's where all your messages land. Here's what you'll find when you open it:

- **Unread Messages:** These are emails you haven't looked at yet. They usually appear in bold text, like unopened letters waiting for you.

- **Folders:** Most email services have folders such as:

  - **Sent:** This is where you'll find emails you've already sent.

  - **Drafts:** If you start an email but aren't ready to send it yet, it will be saved here.

  - **Spam:** This is where suspicious or unwanted emails go, like junk mail. Your email service usually filters these out for you.

Tips for Creating a Strong Password

Your password is key to keeping your email secure. Here are some tips to help you make a good one:

- Use a mix of letters (both uppercase and lowercase), numbers, and symbols.

- Avoid using personal information like your name or birthday.

- Change your password every few months to keep your account secure.

- Use a **password manager** (like 1Password or Google Password Manager) to safely store and remember your passwords for you.

A Few Helpful Tips for Using Your New Email Account

Now that you've got your email set up, here are some tips to help you use it effectively:

- **Check Your Inbox Regularly:** Just like checking your mailbox, it's a good idea to look at your email daily so you don't miss important messages.

- **Delete Spam:** You might receive strange or unexpected emails. These are called spam, and it's best to delete them without opening them.

- **Organize Your Inbox:** Create folders or labels to keep your emails organized, like sorting letters into different drawers. You can also set up filters to automatically sort messages for you.

- **Replying to Emails:** If you get an email, simply click "Reply" to respond. It's like writing back to a letter, only much faster.

- **Watch Out for Scams:** Be cautious if an email asks for personal information, especially if it sounds urgent or too good to be true. If you're unsure, don't hesitate to ask a trusted friend or family member for help.

Final Thoughts

You've done an amazing job setting up your email account! Take a moment to celebrate this achievement. You've unlocked a powerful tool to stay connected, informed, and engaged. Remember, it's okay to take your time and explore your new email account at your own pace. You've got this, and I'm here cheering you on every step of the way!

THE ART OF TEXTING

A FRIENDLY GUIDE TO STAYING CONNECTED ONE MESSAGE AT A TIME

Welcome to the World of Texting

Welcome to the world of texting! Text messaging is one of the quickest and easiest ways to stay connected with friends and family. It's perfect for sending a quick hello, asking a question, or sharing a funny picture—all from your mobile phone. In this chapter, we'll explore what texting is, how it works, and why it's such a wonderful tool for staying in touch. Don't worry—I'll guide you through every step of the way.

What Is Texting?

Think of texting like passing notes or sending postcards, but instead of writing on paper, you type your message on your phone. And instead of waiting days for it to arrive, your message is delivered instantly. Texting is great for letting someone know you're thinking about them or simply saying, "Hi!" without the formality of an email or a phone call.

Most smartphones come with a built-in messaging app that you can use to send and receive texts. It's a simple and fun way to stay connected, whether you're sharing news, having a quick chat, or just sending a smiley face to make someone's day.

The Basics of Texting

Texting is quick, convenient, and easy to learn. Let's break it down:

1. **Short Messages:** Most text messages are just one or two sentences. Think of it like sending a quick note rather than writing a long letter.

2. **Instant Delivery:** Texts are delivered right away, so you can have fast conversations with friends and family, no matter where they are.

3. **Phone Number as Your Address:** Your phone number acts like your mailing address for texts. If someone has your number, they can send you a message.

4. **Works Over Wi-Fi or Mobile Network:** Texting usually uses your mobile network, but some apps also work over Wi-Fi. This is handy if you're in an area with limited cell service.

Why Is Texting So Useful?

Texting has become one of the most popular ways to communicate because it's so simple and versatile. Here's why people love it:

- **Quick Responses:** Texting is perfect when you need a fast answer, like checking what time someone will arrive or asking if they need anything from the store. Send a quick text, and they can reply whenever they're available.

- **Less Formal:** You don't need to worry about starting with "Dear so-and-so" or signing your name at the end. It's like chatting with a friend—just type your message and hit send.

- **Convenient:** Your text messages are always right there on your phone, ready whenever you need them. There's no need to log in or remember a password.

- **Great for Staying Connected:** A quick "Good morning" or "Thinking of you" text can brighten someone's day. It's a simple way to show you care, even if you don't have time for a long conversation.

Adding a Personal Touch to Your Texts

Texting is more than just words—it's a way to add a little fun and personality to your conversations. Here's how you can make your messages even more special:

- **Emojis:** These tiny pictures are a fun way to express your feelings. You can send a smile , a heart , or a thumbs-up to show approval. Emojis add a bit of flair and help convey emotions that words alone might not capture. To use an emoji, open your messaging app and look for the smiley face icon on your keyboard. Tap it to see the emoji menu, then tap the one you want to add to your message.

- **GIFs:** GIFs are short, looping video clips—like little animated pictures. They're great for sharing a laugh or adding a bit of personality to your texts. To send a GIF, look for the GIF button in your messaging app, often near the emoji button. Browse the library or use the search bar to find a GIF that matches what you want to say. Tap on the one you like, and it will appear in your message.

- **Voice Messages:** Sometimes, it's easier to speak than type. With voice messages, you can record a short audio clip instead of writing a text. It's perfect if you're in a hurry or want the recipient to hear your voice. To send a voice message, press and hold the microphone icon near the text box while you speak, then release it to send.

Understanding Common Text Abbreviations

Texting often involves abbreviations to keep messages short and sweet. Here are some common ones you might see, and don't worry—it's okay if they're new to you. You'll get the hang of them quickly!

- **LOL:** Laughing Out Loud (when something is funny)

- **BRB:** Be Right Back (if you need to step away briefly)

- **OMG:** Oh My Gosh (expressing surprise)

- **BTW:** By The Way (adding extra information)

- **TTYL:** Talk To You Later (saying goodbye)

- **IDK:** I Don't Know (when you're unsure)

- **FYI:** For Your Information (sharing helpful info)
- **IMO:** In My Opinion (expressing your thoughts)

Remember, it's perfectly okay to ask if you don't understand one of these. We all learn something new every day!

Staying Safe While Texting

Texting is a great way to stay in touch, but it's important to be cautious. Here are some tips for staying safe:

- **Don't Share Personal Information:** Avoid sending sensitive details like your Social Security number, bank info, or passwords via text.
- **Be Careful with Unknown Numbers:** If you get a text from a number you don't recognize, be cautious. Scammers sometimes pretend to be someone they're not. If a message feels suspicious, it's best to ignore or delete it.
- **Block Unwanted Messages:** If you receive spam texts or messages from someone you don't want to hear from, you can block their number in your messaging app.

Texting Etiquette: Do's and Don'ts

Just like with any form of communication, there are a few good practices to keep in mind when texting. Here are some tips for polite texting:

Do:

- **Keep It Short:** Texting is meant for quick notes. If you have a lot to say, consider calling or emailing instead.

- **Respond When You Can:** It's okay to take your time replying. Texting is often casual, so don't feel pressured to respond immediately.

- **Use Punctuation:** Even though texts are informal, using punctuation helps make your message clearer.

Don't:

- **Avoid USING ALL CAPS:** It can come across as shouting unless you're really excited.

- **Limit Multiple Messages:** Sending several texts in a row can be overwhelming. Try to say everything in one or two messages.

- **Respect Quiet Hours:** Avoid texting late at night unless it's urgent. People have different schedules, and it's best not to disturb their rest.

Final Thoughts

You've made it through the chapter—well done! Texting is a simple yet powerful way to stay connected with loved ones. It might feel a bit tricky at first, but with practice, you'll be texting with confidence in no time. Remember, every small victory counts, and you're doing great!

So grab your phone, open your messaging app, and send a quick hello to someone you care about. You're mastering the art of texting, one message at a time. I'm here cheering you on every step of the way!

Bringing Loved Ones Closer with Video Calls

A Beginner's Guide to FaceTime, Popular Apps, and Making Every Call Count

Welcome to the World of Video Calls

Video calling is a fantastic way to stay in touch with friends and family, especially when you can't be there in person. It's the next best thing to being in the same room—you can see someone's face, hear their voice, and share special moments together, no matter where they are in the world. In this chapter, we'll explore what video calls are, why they're so special, and how they can help you feel closer to the people you care about.

What Is a Video Call?

A video call is just like a regular phone call, but with one big difference—you can see the person you're talking to on your screen. It's a digital face-to-face conversation, almost like sitting across the table from someone, even if they're miles away. Video calls use the internet to connect you with friends, family, or anyone else you want to talk to while allowing you to see their expressions and smile.

Video calls have become incredibly popular, especially when in-person visits aren't possible. They're perfect for celebrating birthdays, catching up with friends, or simply seeing the smile of a loved one who lives far away. It's like having a visit without leaving your home!

How Does Video Calling Work?

Video calls use your device's camera and microphone to connect you with someone over the internet. Here's a simple breakdown:

- **Camera:** The camera on your smartphone, tablet, or computer takes a live video of you and sends it to the person on the other end.

- **Microphone:** Your device's microphone picks up your voice so the other person can hear you clearly.

- **Screen:** The screen shows a live video of the person you're calling, letting you see each other in real time.

You can talk, laugh, and share stories just like you would on a regular phone call, but with the added joy of seeing each other's faces. It's the closest thing to being there in person!

Why Are Video Calls So Special?

Video calls have a unique way of bringing people closer, even when distance makes it hard to visit. Here's why they're so special:

- **See the People You Love:** There's something magical about seeing someone's face while you talk. You can catch their expressions, share a smile, or even see them laugh. It makes the conversation feel warmer and more personal.

- **Share Special Moments:** Video calls are perfect for celebrating important occasions like birthdays, anniversaries, or family gatherings. Even if you can't be there in person, you can still join in the fun and see everyone's happy faces.

- **Stay Connected, No Matter the Distance:** Whether your loved ones are across town or across the world, video calls make it easy to stay in touch. It's a wonderful way to keep up with friends and family, even if you're far apart.

- **Feel Less Alone:** Seeing a familiar face can be incredibly comforting, especially if you're feeling lonely. It's reassuring to know that the people you care about are just a video call away.

Popular Apps for Video Calls

There are many apps available for making video calls, each with its own features. Here are some of the most popular ones:

- **Zoom:** One of the most widely used apps for both one-on-one and group calls. It's great for family get-togethers or virtual parties.

- **Skype:** Skype has been around for a long time and is known for its easy-to-use video calling features. It works well on computers, tablets, and phones.

- **FaceTime:** If you have an Apple device like an iPhone or iPad, FaceTime is a great option. It's simple to use and perfect for calling other Apple users.

- **WhatsApp:** This messaging app also supports video calls. If you already use WhatsApp to chat with friends and family, it's an easy choice for video calls too.

- **Google Meet:** Google Meet is a solid choice for group calls and is easy to use, especially if you already have a Gmail account.

All of these apps are free and provide a great way to see and chat with the people you care about.

Types of Video Calls

There are a few different types of video calls, depending on how many people are involved and what kind of experience you want:

- **One-on-One Calls:** This is the most common type of video call, just between you and one other person. It's perfect for catching up with a friend or chatting with a family member.

- **Group Calls:** Group calls allow you to connect with multiple people at once. It's like having a family reunion, even if everyone is in a different location. These calls are great for celebrating holidays, birthdays, or just spending time together.

- **Virtual Events:** Video calls can be used for special occasions like virtual birthday parties, holiday celebrations, or even online classes. It's a fun way to share experiences together, even when you can't be in the same room.

Tips for a Great Video Call Experience

To make the most of your video calls, here are some helpful tips:

- **Check Your Internet Connection:** A stable internet connection is key for a smooth video call. If your connection is slow, the video may freeze or the sound might cut out. Try to stay close to your Wi-Fi router or use a wired connection if possible.

- **Find a Quiet Spot:** Choose a quiet place for your call to minimize background noise. This will help you and the person you're talking to hear each other clearly.

- **Good Lighting:** Make sure there's enough light for the other person to see you clearly. Natural light from a window works well, or you can use a lamp if it's darker.

- **Position Your Device:** Place your phone, tablet, or computer on a stable surface, and keep the camera at eye level. This way, the person you're talking to can see you easily.

- **Use Headphones:** If you're having trouble hearing or there's a lot of noise around you, headphones can help make the call clearer.

Staying Safe During Video Calls

Just like with any online activity, it's important to stay safe while video calling. Here are some tips to keep in mind:

- **Only Answer Calls from People You Know:** If you receive a video call from someone you don't recognize, it's best not to answer. Stick to calls from people you know and trust.

- **Don't Share Personal Information:** Avoid discussing sensitive information like your bank details or passwords during a call, especially if you're in a group call.

- **Use a Secure Connection:** Keep your video calling app updated and choose apps that have strong security features to help protect your privacy.

How to Make a FaceTime Call: Step-by-Step Guide

Let's try making a video call using **FaceTime**, a popular app for Apple devices like iPhones, iPads, and Mac computers. FaceTime is easy to use and a great choice if you and the person you're calling both have Apple devices. I'll guide you through each step. And if you'd like to learn about other apps like Zoom or Skype, you can find step-by-step guides on our website.

Getting Started with FaceTime

1. **Open the FaceTime App:** Look for the green FaceTime icon on your iPhone, iPad, or Mac. It might be on your Home screen or inside the "Utilities" folder. Tap it to open the app.

2. **Find the Person You Want to Call:**

    - Start typing the name, phone number, or email address of the person you want to call. If they're saved in your Contacts, their information should appear automatically.

- You can also use the **Create Link** feature to schedule a FaceTime call. This option allows you to share a link for a future call, making it easy to plan ahead.

3. **Start the Call:**

    - Tap the **Video** button for a video call or the **Audio** button if you prefer just to talk without video. If you start with an audio call, you can switch to video at any time by tapping the video camera icon.

4. **Wait for Them to Answer:** The call will ring on their end, just like a regular phone call. Once they pick up, you'll see their face on your screen, and they'll see yours. Say hello and enjoy your chat!

Tips for Using FaceTime

- **Switch Between Cameras:** If you want to show something other than your face (like a pet or the view outside your window), tap the **camera flip icon** on your screen to switch to the back camera.

- **Use the Mute Button:** If you need to mute your microphone temporarily, tap the **mute icon**. Tap it again to unmute when you're ready to speak.

- **Try Portrait Mode:** If you want to blur the background behind you, turn on **Portrait Mode** during the call. This helps keep the focus on your face. Look for the Portrait Mode icon when the call starts and tap it to enable.

Troubleshooting Tips

- **Can't See the Other Person?** Make sure both of you have a strong internet connection. If the video is frozen or blurry, try moving closer to your Wi-Fi router.

- **Not Hearing Sound?** Check the volume on your device and try using headphones for better sound quality. You can also take advantage of **Spatial Audio**, which creates a more natural sound experience, especially with headphones.

- **Switch Between Devices:** If you're using multiple Apple devices, you can easily switch between them during a call. For example, if you start the call on your iPhone, you can continue it on your iPad or Mac.

Compatibility Note

FaceTime works on Apple devices running iOS 15 or later and macOS Monterey or later. To use all of the latest features like Portrait Mode and Spatial Audio, make sure your device is updated to the most recent software version.

Where to Learn More

FaceTime is a great way to get started with video calls, especially if you're already comfortable with your Apple device. If you'd like to learn how to use other popular video calling apps like **Zoom**, **Skype**, or **Google Meet**, visit our website for detailed, step-by-step guides tailored just for you.

Final Thoughts

Video calls are a wonderful way to stay connected with the people you care about, whether you're catching up with friends, celebrating a special occasion, or just checking in with family. They let you see familiar faces, hear laughter, and share special moments—even from miles away.

It's okay if it feels a bit intimidating at first. Like any new skill, it takes practice. The more you use video calling, the more comfortable it will become. Before you know it, it will feel as natural as making a regular phone call.

So open your video calling app and give it a try. Connect with a loved one, tell a story, or just say hello. You're doing fantastic, and each call is another step toward mastering this wonderful way to stay in touch.

DIGITAL PHOTOS

DIGITAL GRANDSON PRESS

Mastering Digital Photography

A Friendly Guide to Taking Great Photos with Your Digital Device

Welcome to the Wonderful World of Digital Photography

Digital photography is a fantastic way to capture moments big and small, and it's easier than ever with the camera right in your smartphone, tablet, or digital camera. In this chapter, we'll explore what digital photos are and share some simple tips to help you take great pictures with your device. Whether you're just starting out or already familiar with snapping photos, you'll find that taking good pictures can be a lot of fun once you learn a few basics. Let's dive in together!

What Are Digital Photographs?

A digital photo is a picture taken electronically with a device like a smartphone, tablet, or digital camera. Unlike traditional photos taken on film, digital photos are saved as files on your device, making it easy to view, edit, and share them whenever you want.

Digital photos are made up of tiny dots called **pixels**, and the more pixels a photo has, the clearer and sharper it will be.

> **Pixels:** Pixels are the tiny colored dots that make up the images you see on your screen. Think of them like the pieces of a jigsaw puzzle—the more pieces you have, the more detailed and beautiful the picture will be.

Taking Photos on Your Digital Device

Taking photos with your smartphone, tablet, or digital camera is simple once you get the hang of it. Here are some helpful tips to get you started:

Portrait vs. Landscape Orientation

- **Portrait Mode:** Hold your device vertically. This is best for taking pictures of people or tall objects like trees and buildings.

- **Landscape Mode:** Hold your device horizontally. This is great for capturing wide scenes like sunsets, group photos, or landscapes.

Tip: Think about what you want to capture before deciding on the orientation. If you're photographing a group of friends, landscape mode will help fit everyone into the frame. And don't worry if you accidentally take a sideways picture—we've all been there! You can always rotate it later.

Front-Facing vs. Back-Facing Cameras

Most smartphones and tablets have two cameras:

- **Front-Facing Camera:** This camera is on the same side as your screen and is great for selfies or video calls. It's perfect for snapping a quick photo of yourself when you want to be in the shot.

- **Back-Facing Camera:** Located on the back of your device, this camera usually has better quality. It's ideal for most of your photos, especially when you want a sharp, clear image.

Pro Tip: When taking photos of people, use the back-facing camera for better quality, but don't be afraid to switch to the front camera for a fun selfie moment!

Getting to Know Your Camera App

Take a few moments to explore the camera app on your device. Most apps are designed to be easy to use, with buttons for taking photos, switching between cameras, and adjusting settings. Here's a quick look at what these buttons do:

- **Shutter Button:** This is the large circular button at the bottom of your screen. It's your "go" button for taking a picture—just tap it to snap a photo!

- **Switch Camera Button:** Shown as two arrows forming a circle, this button lets you toggle between the front and back cameras. Use it when you want to take a selfie or switch back to the main camera.

- **Flash Button:** This icon looks like a lightning bolt. Tap it to turn the flash on, off, or set it to automatic. The flash can help in low-light situations, but it's best used sparingly—it can sometimes create harsh lighting.

- **Settings (Gear Icon):** Tap this icon for more advanced settings, like adjusting the photo resolution or enabling HDR (High Dynamic Range). **HDR** helps balance the bright and dark areas in your photo, making it look more natural—especially helpful in tricky lighting.

- **Timer Button:** Set a delay (usually 3 or 10 seconds) before the camera takes the picture. This is great for group shots where you want to get in the photo yourself.

- **Grid Lines Button:** Turning on grid lines can help you line up your shot using the "rule of thirds," which makes it easier to create balanced, well-framed pictures.

- **Zoom Slider:** You can zoom in and out using a slider or by pinching the screen. Be cautious—using digital zoom can make your photo look blurry. It's usually better to move closer to your subject instead.

- **Mode Selector:** Camera apps often have different modes like Photo, Video, Portrait, and Panorama. Make sure you're in **Photo Mode** for regular pictures.

Tips for Taking Great Photos

Focus on Your Subject

Make sure your camera is focused on what you want to capture. Most smartphones allow you to tap the screen where you want the focus to be. If you're photographing a person, tap on their face. This helps the camera adjust the focus and brightness, ensuring your subject looks their best.

Avoid Using Zoom

It can be tempting to zoom in, but using digital zoom often lowers the quality of your photo, making it appear grainy. Instead, try to move closer to your subject for a sharper image. Remember, you can always crop the photo later if needed.

Experiment with Lighting

Good lighting makes a big difference in your photos. Natural light is often the best choice, so if you're indoors, try to position yourself near a window. When you're outside, avoid direct sunlight on people's faces—it can create harsh shadows. Instead, look for shaded areas or take photos during the early morning or late afternoon when the light is softer.

Try This: Play around with different lighting. Take the same photo in sunlight, shade, and indoors to see how the lighting changes the look of your picture. It's a fun way to learn!

Have Fun with Your Photos

The best part about digital photography is that you can take as many photos as you want without worrying about wasting film. Don't be afraid to experiment with different angles or try new techniques. Remember, it's not about getting a perfect picture—it's about capturing moments that matter to you.

Final Thoughts

Digital photos are a wonderful way to save memories, share experiences, and express your creativity. Each picture you take isn't just an image—it's a piece of your story, a memory preserved. Whether it's a grandchild's smile or a beautiful sunset, your photos tell the story of your experiences.

So grab your phone or camera and start exploring. Take a walk, look for interesting things to capture, and have fun seeing the world through your lens. You're doing a fantastic job, and every photo you take is a step toward becoming more comfortable with digital photography. I can't wait to see what you'll capture next!

Organizing Your Digital Memories

How to Easily View, Organize, and Enjoy Your Digital Collection

Enjoying and Organizing Your Digital Photos

Congratulations! You've captured some wonderful digital photos, and now it's time to enjoy them. In this chapter, we'll go over how to view and organize your photos so they're easy to find and share whenever you want. Just like putting together a photo album or framing your favorite snapshots, organizing your digital photos will help you build a beautiful collection of memories to look back on and share with loved ones. Let's dive in together!

Viewing Your Photos

Your device makes it simple to look through all the photos you've taken. Whether you're using a smartphone, tablet, or digital camera, your photos are saved in one central spot. Here's how to get started:

1. **Find Your Photos App:** Most smartphones and tablets have a built-in app for viewing photos. It's usually called **Photos** or **Gallery**, and the icon might look like a flower or

a picture frame. To open it, just tap the icon—consider it your digital photo album!

2. **Browse Your Photos:** Once you've opened the app, you'll see all your photos organized by the date they were taken. You can scroll through your collection just like flipping through a photo album—swipe up or down to see more images.

3. **Tap to View:** Want to take a closer look? Just tap on a photo, and it will open up in full screen. From there, you can swipe left or right to see the next or previous photo. It's like holding a photo in your hands, but you can zoom in for even more detail!

4. **Zoom In and Out:** If you want to focus on a specific part of a photo, place two fingers on the screen and spread them apart to zoom in. To zoom out, pinch your fingers together. This is perfect for getting a closer look at someone's smile or reading a sign in the background.

Tip: Don't be afraid to zoom in and explore the details. It's like looking at a photo under a magnifying glass—there's always something new to discover!

Organizing Your Photos

Now that you know how to view your photos, let's talk about organizing them. Keeping your digital photos organized is like sorting through a box of old pictures or making a scrapbook—it helps you find your favorite moments more easily. Here are some simple and fun ways to organize your photo collection:

1. Create Albums

What Are Albums? Think of digital albums as photo books on your device. You can group related photos together, like those from a vacation, a family gathering, or a special event.

How to Create an Album: Open your Photos app and look for the **Albums** or **New Album** button. Tap it, give your album a name (such as "Family Visit" or "Beach Vacation 2024"), and then select the photos you want to include. It's just like putting together a photo book, but without the mess of glue and scissors!

Why Albums Are Useful: Albums make it easy to find specific photos without scrolling through your entire collection. Imagine having all your favorite memories neatly organized and ready to share—just like flipping to your favorite chapter in a storybook.

Try This: Start by creating an album for a recent event, like a family gathering. It's a fun way to relive the day, and you'll have all your favorite moments in one place.

2. Mark Your Favorites

Highlight Your Best Photos: Most Photos apps let you mark certain photos as favorites by tapping a small heart icon or star. It's like pinning your favorite snapshots on the fridge—always there for a quick smile when you need it.

View Your Favorites: Once you've marked photos as favorites, you can find them all in one place by visiting the **Favorites** section of your Photos app. It's a quick way to access your most cherished moments without searching through your whole library.

Pro Tip: Make it a habit to mark your favorites as you go. That way, you'll have a collection of your best-loved photos ready whenever you want to share them.

3. Delete Unwanted Photos

Keep Only the Best: Digital photography allows us to take as many photos as we want, but not every picture is a winner. You might have a few blurry shots or photos where someone blinked. Spend a little time going through your collection and deleting the ones you don't need. This keeps your library tidy and frees up space on your device.

How to Delete a Photo: Open the photo you want to delete and look for the **trash can icon**. Tap it, and the photo will move to the **Recently Deleted** folder. If you change your mind, you usually have a few days to restore it before it's gone for good.

Encouragement: Don't worry about deleting photos—think of it as making room for more great pictures. And remember, you can always take more!

4. Add Tags or Descriptions

Using Tags: Some Photos apps let you add tags or descriptions to your photos. It's a great way to keep track of who's in the picture, where it was taken, or why it's special. For example, you might tag all photos from a birthday party with "Birthday 2024" to make them easier to find later.

Search with Tags: Once you've added tags, you can easily find photos by typing the tag name into the search bar. It's like using an index in a photo album—you get straight to the pictures you're looking for.

Try This: Start by tagging a few of your favorite photos with simple labels like "Family," "Travel," or "Pets." It's a fun way to organize your memories and makes them easier to find.

5. Explore More Features

Every Photos app has its own special features. For example, on Apple devices, the Photos app can automatically group pictures by recognizing faces or sorting them by location. Spend a little time exploring your app—you might discover tools that make organizing even easier.

Tip: Treat this like a mini-adventure. Tap around, try new features, and see what you like. It's a great way to get more comfortable with your Photos app.

Final Thoughts

Organizing your digital photos is a bit like creating a scrapbook or sorting through a beloved photo box—it can be a relaxing and joyful way to revisit your favorite memories. By making albums, marking favorites, and tidying up your collection, you're not just organizing pictures—you're building a treasure trove of memories for yourself and your loved ones to enjoy.

Take your time and enjoy the process. There's no rush, and there's no right or wrong way to do it—whatever feels best for you is perfect. So grab your phone or tablet, open your Photos app, and start exploring. You've already done a wonderful job capturing these moments, and now you're making it even easier to revisit and share them.

You're doing amazing work, and I can't wait to see how beautifully you organize your photo collection. Each step you take is helping to create a special place for your digital memories. Enjoy the journey, and happy organizing!

Sharing Your Special Moments

A Friendly Guide to Sharing Pictures Across Text, Email, and More

Now that you've captured some wonderful photos and organized them beautifully, it's time to share those special moments with the people you care about. Sharing photos is a fantastic way to spread joy and connect with loved ones. Whether you're sending a quick snapshot to a friend or creating a digital album for your family to enjoy, I'm here to guide you through it step by step.

5 Simple Ways to Share Your Photos

1. Share via Text Message

Why It's Great:

- Quick and personal—perfect for sending a photo directly to a friend or family member.
- Feels like sharing a moment over coffee or passing a photo across the table.

How to Do It:

1. Open the **Photos** app and tap on the photo you want to share.

2. Tap the **share icon** (an arrow pointing up or three dots connected by lines).

3. Choose **Messages** and select the contact you want to send the photo to.

Pro Tip:

- Some messaging apps may reduce the quality of your photos. For the best quality, try using apps like **iMessage** or **WhatsApp**, which keep the images looking sharp.

2. Share via Email

Why It's Great:

- Ideal for adding a personal touch with a longer message.
- It's like sending a digital postcard with a picture and a note.

How to Do It:

1. In your **Photos** app, tap the **share icon** and choose **Email**.

2. Enter the recipient's email address.

3. Add a message if you'd like, such as why this photo made you think of them.

Tip:

- Most email services have a size limit for attachments

(about 25MB). If your photos are too large, try sharing a link from a cloud service like **Google Drive** or **iCloud**.

3. Share on Social Media

Why It's Great:

- Perfect for sharing your favorite moments with a wider circle of friends and family.

- Feels like putting your favorite picture on the fridge for everyone to see.

How to Do It:

1. Open your social media app (e.g., **Facebook** or **Instagram**).

2. Tap the button to create a new post, then tap the photo icon.

3. Choose the photos you want to share and add a caption (e.g., "Had a wonderful day at the park!").

Pro Tip:

- Check your privacy settings before posting, especially if the photos include other people. You can choose to share with just your friends or create a custom list for more control.

4. Create a Shared Album

Why It's Great:

- A wonderful way to share a group of photos with family and friends.

- It's like creating a digital family album that everyone can add to.

How to Do It:

1. Open your **Photos** app and create a **new album**.

2. Select the option to **share** the album.

3. Invite family members by entering their email addresses. Once they accept, they can view the album and add their own photos.

Try This:

- Start a shared album for a recent family gathering. It's a fun way to see everyone's pictures in one place and relive the memories together.

5. Use Cloud Services

Why It's Great:

- Store your photos online and easily share them with others, without worrying about file sizes.

- It's like having a digital safety deposit box for your pictures—you can access them anytime, anywhere.

How to Do It:

1. Open your cloud service app (e.g., **Google Photos**, **iCloud**, or **Dropbox**).

2. Upload the photos you want to share (look for an icon like an upward arrow or plus sign).

3. Tap the **share icon** and choose **Get Link** or **Share Album**.

4. Copy the link and paste it into a text message, email, or social media post.

Tip:

- Double-check the sharing permissions to ensure only the people you want can see the photos. Set the link to "view-only" for added privacy.

Helpful Tips for Sharing Photos

Here are a few reminders to make sharing photos a joyful experience:

- **Pick Your Best Shots:**
  Choose the photos that best capture the moment. Think of it like selecting the perfect picture for a frame.

- **Add a Personal Touch:**
  Include a short note or caption. A simple message like "This reminded me of you!" can make someone's day.

- **Respect Privacy:**
  Always check with the people in your photos before sharing them publicly, especially on social media. It's thoughtful

to ask first.

- **Be Mindful of What You Share:**
  Remember, once a photo is shared online, it's hard to take it back. Make sure you're comfortable with the picture being out there for others to see, just like you would if you were hanging it on a wall.

Final Thoughts

Sharing photos is all about connecting with the people you love and inviting them into the moments that made you smile. Whether it's through a quick text, a heartfelt email, or a shared album, each photo you share is a little gift, a way of saying, "I wish you were here."

There's no right or wrong way to share your photos—whatever feels best for you is the perfect choice. You're building beautiful bridges with every photo you send, and that's something truly special.

So go ahead—send that favorite snapshot, share a lovely memory, or create a digital album for your family. You're bringing joy and connection with every photo, and I'm so proud of the steps you're taking to explore and enjoy the digital world.

You're doing an amazing job, and I can't wait to see all the wonderful moments you choose to share!

STAYING ORGANIZED

DIGITAL GRANDSON PRESS

Handy Helpers

How to Use Calendars, Reminders, and Notes for a Smoother Day

In this chapter, we'll explore some of the most useful tools on your phone or computer that can help you stay organized. Think of these tools as your own personal assistants, always ready to help you keep track of appointments, make to-do lists, or plan your week. Let's dive in and see how these digital helpers can make your life a little easier and more enjoyable!

Overview of Organizational Tools

1. Calendars: Your Digital Datebook

A digital calendar is like the trusty wall calendar you used to hang in the kitchen, but with a few extra perks. You can easily add events, set reminders, and even get notifications so you'll never forget a birthday, appointment, or lunch date again. It's like having a personal assistant who keeps your schedule in check!

When to Use Your Calendar:

- **Scheduling family gatherings or events.**

- **Keeping track of appointments and meetings.**

- **Setting reminders for birthdays and special occasions.**

Tip:
If you have a regular event, like a weekly exercise class or a monthly book club, set it to repeat automatically. It's like having a built-in reminder that does all the remembering for you!

2. Reminders: Your Digital Sticky Notes

Reminders are like little digital sticky notes that keep you on track. Whether it's a nudge to take out the trash, pick up milk, or call a friend, reminders can give you a gentle prod at just the right time. It's like having a friendly voice saying, "Don't forget this!"

When to Use Reminders:

- **Remembering daily tasks like watering the plants or taking medication.**

- **Keeping track of errands, like stopping by the post office.**

- **Setting reminders for important calls or follow-ups.**

Pro Tip:
You can set reminders based on time or even location. For example, set a reminder that says "Pick up milk" when you arrive at the grocery store. It's like a helpful nudge right when you need it most!

3. Alarms & Timers: Your Personal Timekeepers

Alarms and timers are great for helping you stay on schedule. Whether you need a wake-up call, a reminder to take a break, or help timing dinner in the oven, these features are like having a friend who never forgets the time.

When to Use Alarms & Timers:

- **Setting an alarm to wake up in the morning or for an important appointment.**

- **Using a timer to keep track of cooking or baking.**

- **Reminding yourself to take breaks during the day, especially if you're focused on a project.**

Tip:
If you have a daily medication routine, set a recurring alarm. It's like having a friendly reminder that never lets you miss a dose.

4. Notes: Your Handy Digital Notebook

The Notes app is like carrying around a little notebook in your pocket, but without worrying about losing it. You can jot down recipes, ideas, shopping lists, or anything you want to remember. It's a perfect place to catch all your thoughts, and they're safely stored whenever you need them.

When to Use Notes:

- **Writing down grocery lists or to-do lists.**

- **Saving a recipe you want to try.**

- **Jotting down ideas or reminders for later.**

Pro Tip:
Use your Notes app for everything from a favorite quote to a gift idea for a friend. And if you have a long list, try using bullet points or checklists to keep things tidy. It's like having your own little organizer right at your fingertips!

Making the Most of Your Organizational Tools

Now that you've met your digital helpers, let's look at some ways they can make your daily life a little smoother:

- **Organizing Events:** Use your calendar to schedule family gatherings, birthdays, and appointments. It's like having a personal assistant who helps you keep track of all the important dates.

- **Managing Daily Tasks:** Set reminders for everyday tasks like watering the plants or taking your vitamins. It's like a gentle nudge that keeps you on track, so you don't have to worry about forgetting.

- **Getting Things Done:** Create a to-do list in your Notes app or Reminders app. It helps keep everything in one place, making it easy to check off tasks as you go.

- **Staying on Schedule:** Use alarms and timers to keep track of time, whether it's to check on dinner or take a quick break. It's like having a friend who keeps an eye on the clock for you.

- **Capturing Ideas:** Jot down recipes, thoughts, or shopping lists in your Notes app. It's perfect for those moments when you think, "I need to remember this later!"

Final Thoughts

These organizational tools may seem a bit overwhelming at first, but remember—they're designed to make life simpler, not more complicated. Start small, and try out one tool at a time. Play around with your calendar, set a reminder, or create a note. The more you use them, the more comfortable they'll feel.

And don't worry if it takes a little time to get the hang of it. It's okay to experiment and see what works best for you. Whether you're remembering an appointment, managing daily tasks, or jotting down a great idea, these tools can help you feel more in control and make your day run a bit more smoothly.

You're doing a fantastic job just by trying something new. With a bit of practice, you'll be using these digital helpers like a pro. And remember, staying organized isn't about perfection—it's about making life a little easier so you can focus on the things that truly matter.

You've got this! Keep exploring, keep experimenting, and enjoy the feeling of having your own little team of digital helpers by your side.

Your Digital Datebook

Getting Started with Digital Calendars

Your Digital Datebook: Getting Started with Digital Calendars

Welcome to the wonderful world of digital calendars! If you've ever used a wall calendar or kept an appointment book, then you already have a pretty good idea of how these work—just with a few extra features to make your life easier. The best part? Your digital calendar can give you reminders, so you don't have to remember every detail on your own. It's like having a little helper dedicated to keeping your schedule in check. Let's explore how to use digital calendars on smartphones, tablets, and computers together.

How to Use a Digital Calendar

On a Smartphone or Tablet

Most smartphones and tablets come with a built-in calendar app, like **Google Calendar** on Android devices or **Apple Calendar** on iPhones and iPads. Here's how to get started:

1. **Find the Calendar App:**

Look for the calendar icon on your home screen. It usually looks like a small calendar page with a date on it. If you can't find it right away, don't worry—it's probably tucked in there somewhere between your photos and weather app. Think of it as finding your favorite cookbook in a busy kitchen.

2. **Open the App:**
Tap the calendar icon to open it. You'll see a monthly or daily view of your schedule. It's like flipping open your old paper planner, but now everything is neatly stored in one handy screen.

3. **Add an Event:**

   - Tap the **+** button (usually found at the bottom or top corner of the screen). This is where the magic begins!

   - **Enter Details:** Type in the event name, date, time, and location if needed. It's like jotting down notes in your old planner, but without worrying about smudging the ink.

   - **Set a Reminder:** Scroll down to choose when you'd like a reminder—10 minutes before, an hour before, or even a day in advance. It's like a little nudge from your digital grandson saying, "Hey, don't forget your lunch date!"

   - **Save the Event:** Once you've filled in the details, tap **Add**. Congratulations—you've just added your first digital event! It's like sticking a Post-it note to your brain without the sticky mess.

On a Computer

Using a digital calendar on your computer is similar, but you'll have a larger screen and a bit more space to work with. Here's how:

1. **Open Your Calendar:**

   - If you're using a Windows computer, you might use **Outlook Calendar**.

   - On a Mac, you'll find **Apple Calendar**.

   - For anyone using Google, visit calendar.google.com in your web browser. It's like opening up a big desktop planner, but without the pen smudges.

2. **Add an Event:**

   - Look for a button that says **Create** or **New Event** (usually near the top left). Click on it to start creating your event.

   - **Enter Event Details:** Type in the name, date, time, and any notes about the event. Planning a birthday party? Add a reminder to buy a cake—no more last-minute dashes to the bakery!

   - **Set a Reminder:** Click on the **Reminder** option to decide when you want to be notified. You can even add multiple reminders for really important events, like a countdown to your favorite show's season finale.

3. **Save:**

Click **Save** or **Done** or **Add** to add the event to your calendar. Well done! You've taken a big step towards getting more organized.

Key Features of Digital Calendars

Digital calendars come with handy features that make staying organized a breeze. Let's look at a few of them:

- **Appointments and Events:**
  Just like writing in a paper planner, you can add appointments or events. But instead of flipping through pages, you can quickly glance at your week or month. It's like having a bird's-eye view of your schedule—minus the scribbled-out notes when plans change.

- **Reminders:**
  Ever wished someone could give you a little nudge before an important event? Digital calendars do just that! Set reminders for 10 minutes, an hour, or even a day before your event. It's like having your own personal assistant whispering, "Hey, don't forget your 2 PM appointment!"

- **Recurring Events:**
  Do you have a regular appointment, like a weekly book club or a monthly coffee date? You can set these as recurring events, so you only need to enter them once. Your calendar will automatically add them every time—like magic, but even better because it means less work for you!

- **Sharing Events:**
  Need to coordinate plans with family or friends? You can

easily share events with others. If you're organizing a family dinner, create the event and invite everyone. They'll get the event on their calendars too—no more "I didn't know!" excuses!

- **Color-Coding:**
Many calendar apps let you use different colors for different types of events. For example, you might use blue for doctor's appointments, red for family gatherings, and green for exercise. It's an easy way to see what's coming up at a glance, and it adds a splash of color to your schedule!

Tips for Using Digital Calendars

- **Start Small:**
If you're new to digital calendars, begin by adding just a few important events. It's like dipping your toes in the water before diving in.

- **Set Multiple Reminders:**
For really important events, set two reminders—one the day before and one an hour before. It's like having two safety nets, just in case the first one wasn't enough.

- **Use Color-Coding:**
Brighten up your schedule by using different colors for different types of events. It's both functional and adds a bit of fun to your calendar.

- **Sync Across Devices:**
Make sure your calendar is synced across all your devices—phone, tablet, and computer. This way, any changes

you make will show up everywhere. No more scribbling in multiple places!

- **Explore and Experiment:**
Don't be afraid to tap around and try out different features. You might discover a new favorite way to stay organized. It's all part of the fun!

Final Thoughts

Using a digital calendar takes a little practice, but once you get the hang of it, you'll wonder how you ever managed without one. Whether it's helping you remember birthdays, keep track of appointments, or plan time for the things you love, a digital calendar is like having an extra brain that remembers all the little details.

And remember, it's okay to make mistakes while you're learning—we all do! Each event you add is a step toward feeling more in control and less stressed. You're doing great, and your digital calendar is here to help you every step of the way. Keep going—you're just one click away from making life a bit easier and a lot more organized!

Remembering Made Easy

Using Digital Reminders to Stay on Track

Welcome to the world of digital reminders! If you've ever stuck a sticky note on the fridge or tied a string around your finger to remember something, then you're already familiar with the concept of reminders. Digital reminders work just like those sticky notes—but without the risk of losing them when the cat decides to play with the fridge door. Let's dive in and see how reminders on your smartphone, tablet, or computer can help you stay on top of your tasks and appointments, making life a little easier and stress-free.

Why Use Digital Reminders?

Reminders are perfect for keeping track of things you need to do but don't want to forget. Whether it's taking medication, picking up groceries, or simply remembering to call a friend, reminders act like your own personal assistant, helping you stay organized without the mental juggling. Using digital reminders can free up your mind, giving you peace of mind and allowing you to focus on the present without worrying about missing something important. It's like having a gentle nudge from your digital grandson who never forgets!

Setting Up Reminders on Different Devices

On a Smartphone or Tablet

Most smartphones and tablets come with a built-in reminders app, like **Google Keep** or **Reminders** on iPhones and iPads. Here's how to get started:

1. **Find the Reminders App:**
   Look for an app on your home screen that might say "Reminders" or show a little checkmark icon. It's probably nestled between your other productivity tools—like a digital sticky note pad just waiting to be found.

2. **Open the App:**
   Tap on the icon to open it. You'll see a simple screen that lets you add and view reminders. Think of it as your digital notepad, always ready for a new task.

3. **Add a Reminder:**

   - Tap the **+** button or **New Reminder** button.

   - **Enter the Task:** Type in what you need to remember, like "Water the plants" or "Doctor's appointment at 3 PM." If you want, add a little note for extra details—it's like jotting down a reminder and adding a smiley face for good measure.

   - **Set a Time or Date:** Choose when you'd like to be reminded—at a specific time (like 10 AM tomorrow) or on a particular date. This feature is great for appointments, errands, or recurring tasks.

- **Add a Location Reminder (Optional):** Some apps let you set a reminder for when you arrive at or leave a certain place. For example, you can create a reminder that pops up when you get to the grocery store—"Don't forget to buy eggs!" It's like having a little bit of magic in your pocket.

4. **Save the Reminder:**
Tap **Save** or **Done**. Just like that, you've created your very own digital sticky note, ready to remind you when you need it most.

On a Computer

Using reminders on your computer is just as easy, and it's perfect if you're already at your desk. Here's how:

1. **Open Your Reminders Program:**

   - On a Mac, use the **Reminders** app.

   - On a Windows computer, try **Microsoft To Do** or set reminders within **Outlook**.

2. **Create a New Reminder:**

   - Click on **New Task** or **Add Reminder**.

   - **Enter Details:** Type in what you need to remember, along with the time and any notes. You can also set recurring reminders for tasks like "Take vitamins every morning." It's like having a friendly nudge from your computer, helping you stay on top of things.

3. **Save the Reminder:**
   Click **Save** or **Add**. Your reminder will pop up when you need it, keeping you on track without having to scribble notes all over your desk.

Key Features of Digital Reminders

- **Timed Reminders:**
  Set reminders for a specific time. Whether it's a meeting, a phone call, or taking your medicine, these reminders help ensure you don't miss a beat.

- **Recurring Reminders:**
  Need a regular reminder for tasks like taking medication or watering plants? Set up a recurring reminder—daily, weekly, or even monthly. It's like having a permanent sticky note that never falls off and always pops up when you need it.

- **Location-Based Reminders:**
  These are perfect if you often forget things while you're out. Set a reminder that triggers when you arrive at a certain location. Imagine getting a gentle ping to "Pick up milk" just as you pull into the grocery store parking lot. It's like your phone is reading your mind!

- **Sync Across Devices:**
  Reminders set on one device can sync across all your devices. Add a reminder on your phone, and it will show up

on your computer too. It's like having a little helper follow you wherever you go, keeping your notes handy without needing to carry a notepad.

Tips for Using Digital Reminders

- **Keep It Simple:**
  Start with just one or two reminders a day. It can be tempting to set a lot at once, but starting small helps you get comfortable without feeling overwhelmed.

- **Use Voice Commands:**
  Many smartphones let you set reminders using voice commands. Just say, "Hey Siri, remind me to call John at 5 PM," or "Okay Google, remind me to water the plants tomorrow morning." It's like having your very own personal assistant who's always listening—without any eye rolls!

- **Recurring Reminders for Routine Tasks:**
  If you have tasks that happen regularly, like taking medication, set a recurring reminder. You only need to set it once, and it'll keep reminding you—less effort, more results!

- **Customize Notifications:**
  Make sure your reminder notifications suit your needs. Choose sounds that are gentle or loud, depending on how much of a nudge you need. A quiet chime might work for a simple task, but you may want a louder alert for important appointments.

- **Explore and Experiment:**
  Don't be afraid to try out different types of re-

minders—whether it's a time-based one or a location-based alert. You might discover a new favorite way to stay organized. It's like experimenting with new recipes—you never know what might become a new staple!

Final Thoughts

Digital reminders are like little helpers that take the weight off your mind. Whether it's remembering to take your medication, keeping up with appointments, or just reminding you to call a friend, they're here to make life easier. And remember, it's okay to make mistakes as you learn—we're all figuring it out together! With a bit of practice, you'll be setting and using reminders like a pro. You've got this, and your digital reminders are here to support you every step of the way. Keep going—you're well on your way to mastering this handy tool!

TIME ON YOUR SIDE

A GUIDE TO USING DIGITAL ALARMS AND TIMERS

Welcome to the World of Digital Alarms and Timers! If you've ever used an old-fashioned alarm clock to wake up in the morning or a kitchen timer to keep track of dinner, then you already know the basics. The great thing about digital alarms and timers is that they're built right into your devices—no more hunting for that little timer buried in a drawer. Let's explore how these handy tools can help you manage your time on smartphones, tablets, and computers, making life a little easier and stress-free.

Why Use Alarms and Timers?

Alarms and timers are your trusty timekeepers, helping you stay on track throughout the day. Whether it's waking up in the morning, reminding you to take a break, or making sure your cookies don't burn in the oven, these tools are here to help. The best part? They're just a tap away, ready to give you a gentle nudge whenever you need it. Using alarms and timers can take a load off your mind, giving you more freedom to focus on what matters—whether it's enjoying your coffee or spending time with loved ones.

Setting Up Alarms and Timers on Different Devices

On a Smartphone or Tablet

Most smartphones and tablets come with a built-in Clock app that includes alarms and timers. Here's how to get started:

Find the Clock App:
Look for the clock icon on your home screen—it usually looks like an old-fashioned clock face. On iPhones and iPads, use the Clock app. On Android devices, you might see the Google Clock app or a version specific to your phone's manufacturer (e.g., Samsung Clock).

Open the App:
Tap the clock icon to open it. You'll see options like Alarm, Timer, Stopwatch, and World Clock.

Setting an Alarm

1. **Go to the Alarm Section:** Tap on the Alarm tab to see your existing alarms or create a new one.

2. **Add a New Alarm:** Tap the **+** button to add a new alarm.

3. **Set the Time:** Scroll through the numbers to pick the time you want the alarm to go off. It could be 7:00 AM for waking up or 3:00 PM to remind you to call a friend.

4. **Label the Alarm (Optional):** Add a label like "Take Medication" or "Morning Walk." This way, you'll know exactly why the alarm is going off—no more guessing at 6 AM!

5. **Choose a Sound:** Pick a sound for your alarm. It could be a soft melody for waking up gently or a loud buzz for an important reminder. Choose whatever gets you moving in the right direction.

6. **Save the Alarm:** Tap **Save** or **Done**, and your alarm is ready to go. It's like setting a reliable reminder that never misses a beat.

Setting a Timer

1. **Go to the Timer Section:** Tap on the Timer tab in the Clock app.

2. **Set the Duration:** Enter the amount of time you need, whether it's 10 minutes for steeping tea or 30 minutes for your workout.

3. **Start the Timer:** Tap **Start** to begin the countdown. Now you can sit back and relax—your device will let you know when time's up!

On a Computer

You can easily set alarms and timers on your computer too, which is handy if you're spending time at your desk.

Setting an Alarm

1. **Open Your Clock App:**

    ◦ On Windows, use the **Alarms & Clock app**. Note: You

might need to enable notifications to ensure the alarm works even if your computer is asleep.

- On a Mac, use the **Reminders app** or ask Siri to set an alarm for you. Third-party apps like **Wake Up Time** are also good options.

2. **Create a New Alarm:**
Click on **Alarm**, then choose **Add**.

3. **Set the Time and Label:** Enter the time and add a label if you'd like. It's great for reminding you to take a break or stretch while working.

4. **Save the Alarm:** Click **Save** or **Done**. Your computer will now give you a timely alert—no more losing track of time!

Setting a Timer

1. **Use a Timer App:**

   - On Windows, use the timer feature in the **Alarms & Clock app**. Keep the app open or running in the background for the timer to work properly.

   - On a Mac, you can ask **Siri** to set a timer, or use a third-party app.

2. **Set the Timer Duration:** Enter the time you need and hit **Start**. Your computer will count down and notify you when time's up.

Key Features of Alarms and Timers

- **Multiple Alarms:** Set several alarms for different times of the day. Need one for waking up, another for lunch, and one more for an evening walk? No problem! It's like having a row of alarm clocks in one handy app.

- **Custom Labels:** Adding labels helps you remember why the alarm is going off (if supported by your app). Instead of hearing a random beep, you'll see reminders like "Call Sarah" or "Take Vitamins," making it easy to stay on top of your tasks.

- **Custom Sounds:** Choose from a variety of sounds for your alarms and timers. Pick a calming tune for the morning or a louder alert for important tasks. It's your call—literally!

- **Repeat Options:** Set alarms to repeat on certain days, like weekdays only. This is perfect if you need a daily wake-up call but want to sleep in on weekends.

- **Quick Timers:** Timers are great for short tasks, like boiling pasta, timing a nap, or keeping track of your workout. They help you stay focused and save you from constantly watching the clock.

Tips for Using Alarms and Timers

- **Label Your Alarms:** Adding a label makes it clear why the alarm is going off. Instead of wondering what it's for, you'll see exactly what needs your attention.

- **Use Different Sounds:** Choose distinct sounds for different alarms. A soft chime for the morning, a louder tone for midday reminders—this helps you know what each alert is for without even looking.

- **Try Repeat Settings:** For tasks that happen regularly, like taking medication, set the alarm to repeat. You only need to set it once, and it will go off automatically when needed.

- **Use Voice Commands:** You can use voice commands with your device's assistant to set alarms and timers. Try saying, "Hey Siri, set an alarm for 7 AM," or "Okay Google, start a 20-minute timer." You might need to enable voice assistant features on your device first.

- **Experiment and Have Fun:** Don't be afraid to play around with different features—try setting a new sound, or use a timer for a creative task like timing your relaxation breaks. It's your chance to customize these tools and make them your own.

Final Thoughts

Digital alarms and timers are simple but powerful tools for managing your time. Whether you need a wake-up call, a reminder to take a break, or a timer for baking cookies, they're here to make life easier. Don't worry if it takes a little time to get used to them—practice makes perfect! With each alarm you set, you're taking another step toward a smoother, more organized day. You've got this, and your digital devices are here to support you every step of the way. Keep going—you're mastering these helpful timekeepers!

Your Handy Digital Notebook

Getting Started with Digital Notes

Welcome to the world of digital notes! If you've ever jotted down a grocery list on a scrap of paper or scribbled an idea on a napkin, then you already know how helpful notes can be. The beauty of digital notes is that they're always handy—no more worrying about losing that scrap of paper or hunting for a pen in the bottom of your purse. Let's explore how you can use notes on your smartphone, tablet, or computer to keep track of everything from shopping lists to bright ideas.

Why Use Digital Notes?

Digital notes are a fantastic way to capture thoughts, ideas, and reminders without the hassle of keeping track of countless pieces of paper. Whether it's jotting down a recipe, making a list of books you want to read, or saving song lyrics you love, digital notes are your new best friend. The best part? You can access them from multiple devices, so your notes are always where you need them. It's like having a notebook that follows you around everywhere you go!

Getting Started: Setting Up Notes on Your Devices

On a Smartphone or Tablet

Most smartphones and tablets come with a built-in notes app, like **Apple Notes** on iPhones and iPads. For Android devices, **Google Keep** is a popular choice, though you might need to download it from the Google Play Store. Let's dive in and get you set up:

1. **Find the Notes App:**
   Look for an app on your home screen that usually looks like a notepad or a piece of paper. It might be labeled "Notes" or "Keep." If you can't find it, try searching your device's app list.

2. **Open the App:**
   Tap the icon to open your notes app. It's like opening up a little notebook—except this one is always organized, and you can't lose any pages!

3. **Create a New Note:**

   - Tap the **+** button or **New Note** button.

   - **Type Your Note:** Start typing whatever you need to remember—whether it's a shopping list, an idea for a project, or a quick reminder to call a friend.

   - **Formatting Options (Optional):** Many notes apps offer simple formatting like bold text, bullet points, or checklists. Keep in mind that options vary by app—Apple Notes and OneNote have more features, while Google Keep is a bit simpler. Turn your grocery list into a checklist and check items off as you go—no pen required!

- **Save the Note:** Most notes apps save automatically, so you don't need to worry about hitting a save button. Your note will be there when you need it.

On a Computer

Using a notes app on your computer is great for jotting things down quickly while you're at your desk. Here's how:

1. **Open Your Notes App:**

   - On a Mac, use the **Notes** app.

   - On a Windows computer, try **Microsoft OneNote**, the **Windows Notes** app (which syncs with OneDrive), or a simple text editor like **Notepad**.

2. **Create a New Note:**

   - Click on **New Note** or **Add Note** to start a fresh note.

   - **Enter Your Information:** Type in whatever you need—whether it's meeting notes, a recipe, or a reminder.

   - **Organize Your Notes:** If you like staying organized, use folders or tags to keep similar notes together. This can be especially helpful if you have a lot of notes.

3. **Save Your Note:**
   Most notes apps save your notes automatically, but if you're using Notepad or TextEdit, be sure to click **Save** before closing.

Handy Features of Digital Notes

- **Checklists:**
  Turn your note into a checklist—perfect for grocery shopping or packing for a trip. There's something so satisfying about checking items off as you go.

- **Voice Input and Voice Notes:**
  Some notes apps let you use voice input (speech-to-text) or even record voice notes. This is great for when you're in a hurry or prefer speaking over typing. Just talk into your phone, and your thoughts are saved—no typing needed!

- **Sync Across Devices:**
  Notes created on one device can be accessed on another as long as you're signed into the same account (e.g., iCloud for Apple Notes, Google Account for Google Keep, Microsoft Account for OneNote). It's like having your notebook follow you around wherever you go.

- **Add Images:**
  Many apps let you add photos to your notes. This can be helpful for saving a picture of a recipe, a diagram, or anything you want to remember visually.

- **Search Function:**
  Can't remember where you saved that great vacation idea?

Just type a keyword into the search function, and the app will help you locate your note. Some apps can even search through images and attachments!

- **Password Protection:**
  For added privacy, some apps like Apple Notes and OneNote allow you to password-protect your notes. This is great for keeping sensitive information secure.

Tips for Using Digital Notes

1. **Start Simple:**
   Don't overwhelm yourself. Begin with one or two basic notes—like a grocery list or a to-do list—to get comfortable using the app.

2. **Use Checklists:**
   If your app has a checklist feature, take advantage of it for tasks or shopping lists. It's a great way to stay organized, and there's a special kind of satisfaction in checking off each item.

3. **Organize with Folders:**
   If you like things neat and tidy, use folders or tags to categorize your notes. This makes it easier to find what you're looking for later.

4. **Experiment with Voice Notes:**
   Not a fan of typing? Try using voice input or recording a voice note. It's a quick and easy way to capture your thoughts without lifting a finger.

5. **Use the Search Function:**
   With lots of notes, the search function is a lifesaver. Instead of scrolling through endless lists, just type a keyword, and you'll find what you need in seconds.

Final Thoughts

Digital notes are a fantastic way to stay organized and keep track of everything from grocery lists to bright ideas. They're easy to use, always available, and there's no risk of them getting lost in the laundry like the scrap of paper in your pocket. Whether it's a to-do list, a recipe, or a quick reminder, notes are here to make life a little simpler. So go ahead, jot down your thoughts, make those lists, and enjoy the peace of mind that comes with knowing everything you need is just a tap away. Look at you, embracing a new way to stay organized! You've got this, and your digital notes are ready to help every step of the way.

SOCIAL MEDIA

DIGITAL GRANDSON PRESS

Staying Connected

An Introduction to Social Media

Social media has become one of the most popular ways to communicate with friends, family, and even meet new people around the world. It allows us to share experiences, stay informed, and form communities—all from the comfort of our own homes. In this chapter, we'll explore what social media is, look at some of the most common platforms, and learn how to use them to stay connected in fun and meaningful ways.

What is Social Media?

Think of social media as a mix of a bulletin board, a diary, and a community gathering spot, all in one place and right at your fingertips. Social media is a collection of online platforms where people can share photos, videos, messages, and updates with others. It's like having a scrapbook to show your friends, a coffee shop for catching up, and a local newsletter—all rolled into one.

You can share photos of your garden, see what your friends are up to, and even join discussions about topics that interest you. Whether it's sharing a recipe, joining a book club, or simply saying hello to family, social media makes it easier to feel connected—even when you're miles apart.

Popular Social Media Platforms

There are many social media platforms out there, each with its own unique features. Let's go over some of the most popular ones and what they're used for.

1. Facebook

What It Is: Facebook is one of the largest and most widely used social media platforms, especially popular among older adults. It's designed for keeping in touch with friends and family. You can share photos, post updates, join groups, and leave comments on other people's posts.

Why People Use It: It's great for staying in touch with loved ones, joining hobby groups (like gardening or cooking), and keeping up with community events. Think of it as a big, friendly neighborhood where everyone shares what they've been up to.

Tip from the Digital Grandson: If you're just getting started, try posting a photo from your latest trip or leaving a comment on a friend's post. It's an easy way to dip your toes in the water!

2. Instagram

What It Is: Instagram is a visual platform focused on sharing photos and short videos. It's great for seeing beautiful pictures, like snapshots of family celebrations or scenic vacation spots. Instagram has also added Reels—short, entertaining videos similar to what you'd find on TikTok.

Why People Use It: If you enjoy photography or simply like to see what others are sharing, Instagram is a fun and visually engaging platform. You can follow friends, family, and even join communities based on your interests, such as nature photography or home decor.

Tip from the Digital Grandson: Use Instagram's "Close Friends" feature to share more personal moments with a smaller, selected group. It's like passing around a private photo album.

3. X (formerly Twitter)

What It Is: X, previously known as Twitter, is a platform for sharing short updates or posts, known as "tweets." It's like sending a quick note or headline to the world. The platform has evolved, allowing for longer posts, videos, and multimedia content.

Why People Use It: X is popular for staying updated on current events, sharing opinions, and joining conversations on trending topics. It's a great way to follow news, get real-time updates, or see what people are talking about.

Tip from the Digital Grandson: Follow a few trusted news accounts or hobby-related profiles to see content you enjoy without feeling overwhelmed.

4. TikTok

What It Is: TikTok is a platform for sharing short, creative videos. It's full of entertaining content—everything from cooking tips and travel clips to dancing and funny moments. The videos are designed to be quick and engaging, and the app's algorithm does a great job of showing you content based on your interests.

Why People Use It: TikTok is perfect if you like watching short, entertaining videos or want to learn something new in a fun way. You can find videos on practically any topic, from DIY crafts to delicious recipes.

Tip from the Digital Grandson: If you're new to TikTok, start by browsing the "For You" feed, which curates videos based on your preferences. You don't have to post anything right away—just enjoy exploring!

5. WhatsApp

What It Is: WhatsApp is a messaging app used for chatting with individuals or groups. It's a great way to send messages, photos, or videos directly to friends and family. It also features voice and video calls, all with strong privacy protections through end-to-end encryption.

Why People Use It: Many use WhatsApp to stay in touch with loved ones, especially those living abroad. It's like a direct phone line that also lets you share photos and videos easily.

Tip from the Digital Grandson: Create a family group chat to share updates and photos with everyone at once. It's a wonderful way to keep the whole family connected!

How Social Media Keeps Us Connected

Social media is a fantastic way to share your life and stay connected with the people who matter most. Here are some ways you can use it:

- **Share Photos and Videos**: Post a picture of your garden in full bloom or a video of your grandchild's first steps. It's a great way to let others share in your joy.

- **Comment and React**: Leave a comment on a friend's post or tap the "like" button. It's a little gesture that feels like a virtual hug or high five.

- **Join Groups and Communities**: Whether you're interested in local events, cooking tips, or classic movies, there's a group for you. It's a great way to meet people who share your interests and learn something new.

Understanding Social Media Algorithms

Social media platforms use algorithms—like digital librarians—to decide what content to show you based on your preferences. If you like posts about gardening, you might see more gardening tips pop up in your feed.

- **Personalized Feed**: It's like having a custom-made magazine full of articles, photos, and videos tailored just for you.

- **Echo Chambers**: Be mindful that algorithms can sometimes show you only what they think you want to see, limiting different perspectives. It's good to mix things up now and then!

- **Monetizing Your Attention**: Social media platforms often show content that keeps you engaged longer because they make money from ads. If you find yourself scrolling for too long, don't hesitate to take a break!

Staying Safe on Social Media

While social media can be a lot of fun, it's important to stay safe. Here's how:

- **Adjust Privacy Settings**: Take a moment to review who can see your posts. Most platforms let you choose to share only with friends.

- **Protect Your Information**: Avoid sharing sensitive information like your home address or phone number. Remember, social media is a public space.

- **Think Before You Post**: Once something is online, it's hard to take back. Ask yourself if you'd be comfortable with everyone seeing it before you hit "share."

Final Thoughts

Social media can be a wonderful tool for connection and joy. Whether you're sharing a family photo, joining a group, or just scrolling through updates, it's all about feeling closer to the people you care about.

Remember, there's no rush. Take your time, explore the platforms that interest you, and find what feels right for you. I'm here to help, just like I've helped my own grandparents—together, we can make social media a fun part of your daily life.

Welcome to Facebook

Discover How to Set Up, Personalize, and Connect with Loved Ones—One Simple Step at a Time

Welcome to the exciting process of creating a Facebook profile! Facebook is one of the most popular social media platforms, and it's a fantastic way to stay in touch with friends and family, near and far. In this chapter, we'll guide you through setting up your Facebook profile—from choosing a profile picture to writing a brief bio and understanding your privacy settings. Don't worry if this feels a bit overwhelming at first; we'll take it one step at a time, and I'm here to help you every step of the way.

What is Facebook?

Facebook, launched in 2004 by Mark Zuckerberg and his college roommates, was initially created for students but quickly became a platform for everyone. It's now part of **Meta Platforms**, the company behind Instagram, WhatsApp, and Meta Quest (formerly Oculus). Meta aims to connect people and create shared experiences online, including the development of the metaverse—a virtual environment where people can interact digitally.

What is a Facebook Profile?

Think of your Facebook profile as your personal bulletin board—a place where you can pin your favorite photos, share little notes about yourself, and connect with friends and family. It's your online space to express who you are, share what you enjoy, and keep in touch with loved ones.

Together, we'll walk through each part of setting up your profile, making sure you feel confident and comfortable along the way.

Step-by-Step Guide for Creating Your Facebook Profile

1. Create a Facebook Account

Before we set up your profile, you'll need a Facebook account. This step is like filling out a simple registration form at a community club.

- **Enter Your Information**: Visit facebook.com and click "Sign Up." You'll be asked to enter basic information like your name, email address or phone number, and a password. Choose a strong password that's easy for you to remember but hard for others to guess. Try using a mix of numbers, symbols, and words instead of birthdays or pet names.

- **Grandson's Tip**: If you're using a tablet or phone, the sign-up button might look a little different, but don't worry—it's usually at the bottom of the screen.

2. Add a Profile Picture

Your profile picture is like the front door to your profile; it's the first thing people see.

- **Choose a Photo**: Pick a picture of yourself that you like. If you're camera shy, you could use a photo of something meaningful to you, like your garden or a favorite coffee mug.

- **Upload the Photo**: Click the profile picture icon (a small circle). On a desktop, select "Upload Photo"; on a phone or tablet, tap the picture and choose "Edit" or "Upload New Photo." Don't worry if it takes a couple of tries—you'll know the right one when you see it.

3. Add a Cover Photo

The cover photo is like the banner at the top of your profile, adding a bit of personality.

- **What is a Cover Photo?** It's a larger image that sits behind your profile picture. You can use a photo of your favorite place, a beautiful landscape, or a cherished family moment.

- **Upload Your Cover Photo**: Click "Add Cover Photo" on your desktop or tap the cover area on your phone to choose a picture from your device.

4. Write a Bio

Your bio is a brief introduction about yourself, similar to the "About Me" section in a yearbook, but shorter.

- **Keep It Simple**: You only need a sentence or two. For example: "Lover of gardening, good books, and spending time with my grandkids," or "Enjoying retirement and learning new things every day!" You've got 101 characters, so have a little fun with it.

- **Grandson's Tip**: If you're not sure what to write, think about what you'd say if you were introducing yourself to someone new.

5. Adjust Your Privacy Settings

It's important to feel safe and comfortable sharing online. Facebook's privacy settings let you control who can see your profile.

- **Control Who Sees Your Profile**: Access privacy settings through the "Settings & Privacy" menu (look for a gear icon or three horizontal lines). You can decide whether your profile is public or only visible to friends.

- **Grandson's Tip**: Think of this like deciding whether to keep your front door open for everyone or only for close friends.

6. Add Personal Information (Optional)

You can share details like your hometown, school, or favorite hobbies, but only if you feel comfortable.

- **Share What You're Comfortable With**: This information can help old friends recognize you, but it's entirely up to you. You don't need to fill in every detail—just what feels right.

7. Find Friends and Connect

Now that your profile is set up, it's time to start connecting with friends and family.

- **Search for Friends**: Use the search bar at the top of the page. Type in names, and Facebook will suggest people you may know.

- **Send Friend Requests**: Click "Add Friend" to send a request. If they accept, you'll be able to see each other's posts. It's like giving a friendly wave to say hello.

8. Post Your First Update

Share a little something about your day.

- **What's on Your Mind?** Click the box labeled "What's on your mind?" to write a message, share a photo, or link to something interesting. It's like sending a note to your friends about what you're up to.

9. Like Pages and Join Groups

Facebook isn't just for connecting with friends; it's also a place to follow pages and join groups that interest you.

- **Follow Pages**: Pages are like profiles for businesses, public figures, or organizations. Follow The Digital Grandson's Guide to Tech page for helpful tips and updates!

- **Join Groups**: Groups are online communities for people with shared interests, like gardening, classic movies, or travel. It's a great way to meet new people and join conversations.

Using Your Facebook Profile

Your Facebook profile is more than just a collection of photos and facts. It's a place to connect, share, and stay in touch.

- **Like and Comment**: Click the "Like" button if you enjoy a friend's post, or leave a comment to join the conversation. It's like giving a thumbs-up or chatting at a family gathering.

- **Share Photos and Memories**: To share a photo, click "Photo/Video" and select images from your device. It's just like showing friends a photo album, but instant!

- **Join More Groups**: Explore groups based on your interests—whether it's cooking, crafting, or classic films, there's something for everyone.

Final Thoughts

Creating a Facebook profile is like setting up your own personal online space—a place to share your interests, connect with loved ones, and have a little fun. There's no rush, so take your time and enjoy the process. Every step is a chance to learn something new, and remember, I'm right here with you.

So go ahead, upload that profile picture, write a little about yourself, and start connecting. You're doing great, and it's wonderful to see how far you've come. You're just one click away from mastering the digital world, and I'm excited to be part of your journey!

Welcome to Instagram

Let's Create Your Profile and Explore Together

Instagram is a fun, visual way to connect with friends, family, and even new people who share your interests. It's all about sharing photos, videos, and moments that matter to you. In this chapter, I'll guide you through creating an Instagram profile, uploading photos, writing a bio, and using the app to share your favorite moments. If this feels a bit overwhelming, don't worry—I'm here to help you every step of the way.

What is Instagram?

Instagram started in 2010 as an app for sharing photos, and it quickly became popular because it made it easy and enjoyable. Now, Instagram is part of **Meta Platforms**, the same company that owns Facebook. You can use Instagram to share photos, videos, Reels (short videos), and Stories (temporary posts that disappear after 24 hours). It's a great way to stay connected, see what your friends are up to, and discover new content based on your interests.

What Is an Instagram Profile?

Think of your Instagram profile as your own digital scrapbook. It's a place to collect and share photos and videos that mean something to you. You can also write short updates, leave comments, and send messages. Your profile gives people a chance to learn a little about you and what you enjoy. Let's get started with setting up your profile so you can begin sharing and connecting visually.

Step-by-Step Guide for Creating Your Instagram Profile

1. Download the Instagram App

To use Instagram, you'll need the app on your smartphone or tablet.

- **Get the App**: Go to the App Store (for iPhones) or Google Play Store (for Android phones) and search for "Instagram." Tap **Download** or **Install** to add the app to your device.

- **Grandson's Tip**: If you're not sure where the app store is, look for an icon that says **App Store** or **Google Play**—it's like a little shopping bag for apps.

2. Register for an Account

Now let's create your account. This is like signing up for a club—you'll need a few basic details.

- **Create Your Account**: Open the Instagram app and tap

Sign Up. You can register using your email address, phone number, or even connect with your Facebook account if you have one. You can also sign up using your Apple ID or Google account.

- **Choose a Strong Password**: Just like you would for any other account, pick a password that's easy for you to remember but hard for others to guess. Avoid using birthdays or pet names. Instead, try mixing in numbers and symbols.

Grandson's Tip: If you link your Instagram account with Facebook, it can make signing in easier and help you find friends who are already on Instagram.

3. Add a Profile Picture

Your profile picture is the first thing people will see when they visit your Instagram page, so let's choose one that represents you.

- **Choose a Photo**: It could be a nice picture of yourself or something that makes you happy, like a photo of your garden, pet, or favorite coffee mug.

- **Upload the Photo**: Tap the profile icon (it looks like a person's head) in the bottom right corner of the screen. Then, tap **Edit Profile** and select **Change Profile Photo**. You can either upload an existing photo from your device or take a new one.

Grandson's Tip: If the options look a bit different, don't worry—Instagram updates its layout often. Just look for **Edit Profile**, and you'll find it.

4. Write a Bio

Your bio is a short introduction about yourself that appears under your profile picture. It's a quick way to tell others a little bit about you.

- **Keep It Simple and Fun**: Your bio can be up to 150 characters long, so keep it brief. For example, you might write: "Lover of gardening, good books, and spending time with my grandkids," or "Sharing recipes and tips from my kitchen." Feel free to add an emoji or two if it suits your style!

- **Grandson's Tip**: Think of your bio like a friendly introduction at a party—just a few words to give people a sense of who you are.

5. Start Following Friends and Family

Now that your profile is set up, let's connect with friends and family.

- **Find People You Know**: Tap the **Menu** (three horizontal lines) in the top right corner of your profile and select **Discover People** or **Find Friends**. You can search for people by name or connect your contacts to see who's already on Instagram.

- **Connect Through Facebook**: If you have a Facebook account, Instagram can suggest friends who are also on Instagram. Tap **Find Friends** and follow the prompts to connect your accounts.

Grandson's Tip: Following someone is like saying, "I'd love to see what you share!" Don't be shy about following family members or close friends—they'll be happy to connect with you.

6. Share Your First Photo or Video

Let's post something to your profile—it's like adding a favorite photo to your scrapbook.

- **Capture a Moment**: Tap the **plus icon** (usually at the bottom center or top of the screen) to create a new post. You can take a new photo or video, or select one from your device's gallery.

- **Add a Caption**: After choosing your photo, write a short caption. It could be something like, "Enjoying a beautiful day at the park!" or "My latest baking creation." Captions help tell the story behind your photos.

Grandson's Tip: Don't worry about getting it perfect—just share what makes you happy!

7. Explore and Interact

Instagram is all about connection, so let's start exploring and interacting with others.

- **Like and Comment**: If you see a photo you like, tap the **heart icon** below it. You can also leave a comment to say something nice—it's like giving a compliment in person.

- **Follow Hashtags**: Hashtags are like digital labels that help organize posts. If you enjoy gardening, try following hashtags like #gardeningtips or #flowerlove to see related posts. It's a fun way to discover new ideas and connect with people who share your interests.

Grandson's Tip: Think of hashtags as little signs pointing you to content you'll love!

8. Discover New Content with Stories and Reels

Instagram isn't just for photos—there are Stories and Reels, too!

- **Stories**: These are temporary posts that disappear after 24 hours. To share a Story, tap the camera icon in the upper left corner and take a quick photo or video.

- **Reels**: Reels are short, engaging videos, similar to TikTok. You can find them on the Explore page or create your own by tapping the plus icon.

Grandson's Tip: Stories are great for sharing quick updates without cluttering your profile. Reels are perfect if you want to share a fun video moment.

Final Thoughts

Creating an Instagram profile is a wonderful way to share your life and stay connected with loved ones. It's like having a digital scrapbook you can update anytime, filled with moments that bring you joy. There's no right or wrong way to use Instagram—just share what makes you happy and connect in a way that feels natural to you.

So go ahead, add that profile picture, post a photo of something that made you smile today, and start following friends and family. You're doing fantastic, and I'm right here to help you along the way. You're one step closer to mastering the digital world, and it's exciting to see what you'll share next!

Welcome to X (Formerly Twitter)

A Guide to Getting Started and Exploring

X (formerly known as Twitter) is a platform where people can share short updates, called **posts**. These posts can be about anything—your thoughts, a piece of news, or even a funny moment from your day. In this chapter, we'll walk you through setting up your profile, making your first post, and connecting with others in a quick, easy, and enjoyable way.

What Is X?

X is a social media platform that started in 2006 as Twitter. It quickly became a popular place for sharing quick updates and following news in real time. In 2023, the platform rebranded as X, embracing a new vision under the leadership of Elon Musk. Today, X is more than just a site for updates—it's a digital town square where you can connect, learn, and share with the world.

On X, posts are typically limited to **280 characters**—this keeps things short and sweet. However, if you sign up for **X Premium** (a paid subscription), you can write longer posts, sometimes up to **4,000 characters** or more.

Getting Started: Creating Your X Profile

Think of your X profile as your digital introduction. It's where people can learn more about you, see your posts, and stay up to date on what you're sharing. Let's go step by step to set it up.

1. Download the X App

To get started, you'll need the X app on your smartphone or tablet.

- **iPhone users**: Go to the **App Store** and search for "X" or "Twitter" (it may still appear as "Twitter" in some places).

- **Android users**: Open the **Google Play Store** and search for "X" or "Twitter."

Tap **Download** or **Install**, and the app will be added to your device.

2. Register for an Account

Open the X app and tap **Sign Up**. You'll be asked to enter your name, email address (or phone number), and create a password.

- **Tip**: Choose a secure password. Avoid using easy-to-guess options like your birthday or pet's name. A strong password includes a mix of letters, numbers, and symbols.

Think of this as filling out a simple form to get started—it only takes a few minutes.

3. Add a Profile Picture

Your profile picture is the image that represents you on X. It could be a photo of yourself, a favorite hobby, or something that has meaning to you.

- To add your picture, tap the **profile icon** in the upper left corner of the screen, then choose **Edit Profile**. Tap **Change Profile Photo** to select a photo from your device or take a new one.

- **X Premium users**: You also have the option to use an NFT (a special kind of digital image) as your profile picture.

This step helps others recognize you, so pick a photo that feels like you.

4. Write a Short Bio

Your bio is a brief description that appears right below your profile picture. It's a quick way to introduce yourself to others.

- You have **160 characters**, so keep it short and sweet. You might write something like: "Retired teacher, book lover, and proud grandparent," or "Sharing tips on gardening, good food, and family moments."

Feel free to add an emoji or two if that suits your style—emojis can add a bit of personality and fun.

5. Find Friends and Interesting Accounts to Follow

X is all about following people and seeing what they share. You can start by looking up friends and family members using the search bar. Type their names, and you should see their profiles pop up.

- You can also follow accounts based on your interests—whether it's news, cooking, travel, or local events. Following these accounts helps you see posts about topics you enjoy.

- Another way to discover content is by following **Topics**. These are like categories (e.g., Gardening, Music, Current Events) that tailor your feed to show posts related to what you love.

Think of following people and topics as creating your own personalized newspaper.

6. Make Your First Post

A post (what used to be called a "tweet") is a short message you share with your followers. It's like writing a quick note for everyone to see.

- To make your first post, tap the **feather icon** in the bottom right corner of the screen. Type your message (up to 280 characters) and then tap **Post**.

- **Example**: You might say, "Hello, X community! Excited to join and start exploring," or "Enjoying a sunny day at the park—perfect weather!"

Don't worry about being fancy—just share what's on your mind. Your first post is a great way to introduce yourself.

7. Interact and Engage with Others

On X, it's easy to connect with people. Here are some simple ways to interact:

- **Like a post** by tapping the heart icon below it. This is like giving a thumbs-up.

- **Repost** (previously called retweet) if you see something you want to share with your own followers—tap the repost icon, and it will be shared to your feed.

- **Reply** to join the conversation. If someone posts something interesting, tap the speech bubble icon and leave a comment. It's a fun way to chat with others and share your thoughts.

Think of these actions as ways to join in and connect with the community.

8. Explore Hashtags and Communities

Hashtags are words or phrases that start with the **#** symbol (e.g., #GardeningTips, #MondayMotivation). They help group posts about the same topic.

- Clicking on a hashtag shows you all the posts related to it, making it easy to find and join discussions.

- X also has **Communities** and **Spaces**, where you can connect with others who share your interests. Communities are like online clubs, while Spaces are real-time audio chats where you can listen or join in.

Exploring these features is a great way to discover new content and meet people with similar hobbies.

Final Thoughts: Welcome to the Conversation

Creating your X profile is just the beginning. Now you can share your thoughts, stay informed, and connect with others in a friendly and simple way. Remember, it's okay to take your time—exploring X should feel fun, not overwhelming.

As you get started, try making a post, following a few accounts, and liking or replying to things you find interesting. You're already on your way, and I'm here to support you every step of the journey. Welcome to X—you've got this, and I can't wait to see what you share!

ENTERTAINMENT

DIGITAL GRANDSON PRESS

Streaming Simplified: Your Guide to Watching What You Love Online

From Netflix to YouTube, Here's Everything You Need to Know to Get Started

Streaming allows you to watch movies, TV shows, and even live broadcasts over the internet without having to download them first. It's like having an entire library of entertainment at your fingertips, ready whenever you are. Instead of waiting for a whole movie or show to download, streaming lets you start watching right away. It's quick, convenient, and gives you the freedom to watch whatever you want, whenever you want.

In this chapter, we'll explore popular streaming services and walk through the basics of how to get started. Whether you're brand new to streaming or just looking to learn more, I'm here to guide you step by step—just like I would if I were sitting next to you on the couch.

What is Streaming?

Streaming is a way to play video or audio content directly from the internet in real time, without downloading it first. Think of it like turning on the TV or radio: you don't have to wait for the entire program to load before you start enjoying it. As long as you have a steady internet connection, streaming lets you watch movies, shows, or even live events almost instantly.

Many people love streaming because it means no more fussing with DVDs, recording devices, or schedules. You can pause, rewind, and even pick up right where you left off—perfect for when you need to take a break or want to rewatch a favorite scene. Streaming really puts you in control of what you watch.

Popular Streaming Services

There are several streaming services out there, each offering a variety of content. Let's look at some of the most popular ones and what makes them special. Don't worry if it feels like a lot—I'll help you find one that's right for you.

1. Netflix

What It Is: Netflix is one of the largest streaming services, with a wide selection of TV shows, movies, documentaries, and original content you won't find anywhere else.

Why People Love It: Netflix has something for everyone, from comedies and dramas to family-friendly films and thrilling mysteries. It's like having a movie theater, TV network, and library all rolled into one. Just keep in mind that Netflix now requires an extra fee if you want to share your account with someone outside your household.

2. Amazon Prime Video

What It Is: Amazon Prime Video is part of the Amazon Prime membership. It offers a mix of popular movies, TV shows, and Amazon Originals.

Why People Love It: In addition to its large library, Prime Video lets you rent or buy newer releases that might not be included in the regular subscription. It's great if you want to watch a new movie without heading to the theater. Note: Not all Amazon Prime subscriptions include Prime Video in every country, so be sure to check your plan.

3. Disney+

What It Is: Disney+ is a streaming service filled with content from Disney, Pixar, Marvel, Star Wars, and National Geographic. It's a hit with families and fans of classic Disney films.

Why People Love It: Disney+ offers something for everyone, whether you're watching a new Pixar movie with the grandkids or reliving a classic Disney film that brings back childhood memories. In some regions, Disney+ also includes Hulu content as part of a bundle.

4. Hulu

What It Is: Hulu provides a mix of current TV shows, movies, and original series. It's one of the best ways to stay up-to-date with your favorite TV programs.

Why People Love It: Hulu often releases episodes shortly after they air on TV, making it perfect if you want to catch the latest episodes without waiting. Keep in mind that Hulu is only available in the U.S. and Japan, but some of its content may be available on Disney+ in other countries.

5. YouTube

What It Is: YouTube is a platform where people from all over the world share videos on just about everything—cooking, travel, music, education, and more.

Why People Love It: YouTube is free and has an incredible variety of content. Whether you're looking for a tutorial on a new recipe, a music video, or a documentary, YouTube likely has it. If you prefer an ad-free experience, you can subscribe to YouTube Premium.

Getting Started with Streaming

Ready to start streaming? Here's what you'll need:

- A device (smartphone, tablet, computer, smart TV, game console, or streaming device like Roku, Chromecast, or Amazon Fire Stick).

- A stable internet connection (for smooth playback, aim for at least 5 Mbps for HD content and 25 Mbps for 4K).

- Access to a streaming service (we'll help you pick one).

Step 1: Choose a Streaming Service

Decide what type of content you're interested in. Do you enjoy movies, TV shows, or family-friendly content? Based on your preferences, choose a streaming service from the list above.

Install the App: Go to your device's app store, search for the app (e.g., Netflix), and tap **Install**. If you get stuck, don't worry—it's as simple as downloading a game or an email app.

Sign Up: Most streaming services will ask you to create an account. Just enter your email address, choose a password, and follow the prompts. Some services like YouTube are free, while others require a subscription.

Step 2: Explore the App

Browse through the home screen of the app, where you'll see categories like "Recommended for You" or "New Releases." You can also search for specific shows or movies.

Step 3: Start Streaming

When you find something you like, click on it to view the details, then tap **Play**. It's like pressing play on a DVD, but without worrying about scratches or loading screens!

Playback Controls: You can pause, rewind, or fast forward using the on-screen controls. If you're watching on a TV, use your remote. On a computer, use your mouse or trackpad, and on a smartphone or tablet, just tap the screen.

Tips for a Great Streaming Experience

- **Check Your Internet Connection**: If your video keeps pausing to load, it might mean your internet connection is slow. Try moving closer to your Wi-Fi router or restarting it.

- **Use Subtitles**: Having trouble hearing the dialogue? Most streaming services offer subtitles (look for the **CC** icon).

- **Create a Watchlist**: Many services let you save shows and movies to watch later. It's like making a to-do list, but for your entertainment!

The Joy of Streaming

Streaming is a wonderful way to explore a world of entertainment on your terms. Whether you're watching a classic film, discovering a new TV series, or learning something new on YouTube, you have complete control over your experience—no commercials or schedules needed.

If you get stuck or need help, remember I'm right here with you, ready to guide you through it. So grab a snack, find a cozy spot, and let's dive into a relaxing evening of streaming together. You've got this, and I'm here every step of the way!

Your Digital Library: How to Enjoy Books Anytime, Anywhere

A Friendly Guide to Using Reading Apps for a World of Stories at Your Fingertips

Reading has always been a wonderful way to discover new worlds, learn new skills, and unwind. These days, reading apps have made it possible to carry an entire library with you wherever you go. In this chapter, I'll introduce you to some popular reading apps and walk you through the basics of using them. Whether you've been a lifelong book lover or you're just getting back into reading, these apps make it easier than ever to enjoy your favorite stories.

What Are Reading Apps?

Reading apps (short for "applications") are digital tools that let you read books, magazines, and even comics directly from your smartphone, tablet, or computer. Imagine having all of your favorite books in your pocket—no need to carry heavy paperbacks or worry about finding room on your bookshelf. With a reading app, you can access a vast collection of books whenever and wherever you want.

Plus, reading apps let you customize your experience. You can change the font size, bookmark pages, highlight favorite passages, and even take notes—no pen or sticky notes needed! Let's dive into some of the most popular reading apps and how to get started using them.

Popular Reading Apps

There are many reading apps available, each with unique features and book selections. Here are a few favorites:

1. Kindle

What It Is: The Kindle app, created by Amazon, allows you to read eBooks from the Kindle Store. It's one of the most popular reading apps, offering a wide selection of books, magazines, newspapers, and even graphic novels.

Why People Love It: With the Kindle app, you can access thousands of books, from bestsellers to timeless classics. It syncs your progress across devices using Amazon's Whispersync technology, so you can start reading on your tablet and continue right where you left off on your phone. You can also highlight text, take notes, and download books for offline reading—perfect for long flights or car rides.

2. Apple Books

What It Is: Apple Books is a reading app available on iPhones, iPads, and Mac computers. It offers a wide range of eBooks and audiobooks that you can purchase directly through the app.

Why People Love It: Apple Books has a simple, user-friendly interface that integrates smoothly with other Apple services. It's perfect if you already own Apple devices and want a consistent reading experience. You can also use features like Dark Mode for comfortable nighttime reading.

3. Google Play Books

What It Is: Google Play Books is an app available for both Android and iOS devices, as well as on any web browser. It allows you to purchase and read eBooks, audiobooks, and even free public domain classics.

Why People Love It: Google Play Books is versatile, letting you read on any device and switch between eBooks and audiobooks easily. It's a great option if you enjoy reading classic novels without spending a penny—there's a huge selection of free titles.

4. Libby by OverDrive

What It Is: Libby is a library app that connects to your local library, allowing you to borrow eBooks and audiobooks for free, just like you would a physical book.

Why People Love It: Libby is a fantastic choice if you love libraries and want access to a wide range of books without purchasing them. All you need is a library card to get started. The app makes it easy to browse and borrow books, and it even lets you manage multiple library cards if you belong to different libraries.

5. Audible

What It Is: Audible is an app for listening to audiobooks. It's perfect if you prefer to listen to stories while you're on the go or while doing something else, like cooking or exercising.

Why People Love It: Audible offers an extensive selection of audiobooks, and it's great for multitaskers. You can adjust the playback speed, set a sleep timer, and seamlessly switch between listening on your phone or tablet. If you have a Kindle book, Audible's WhisperSync feature can even pick up where you left off in the text.

Getting Started With Reading Apps

To begin using a reading app, you'll need three things: a device (such as a smartphone, tablet, or computer), an internet connection, and access to the app. Let's go through it step by step:

1. Choose a Reading App

Start by deciding what types of books or content you'd like to read. Are you interested in eBooks, audiobooks, or borrowing books from the library? Choose an app that best suits your needs, like Kindle for eBooks, Audible for audiobooks, or Libby for free library books.

Grandson's Tech Tip: If you're unsure which app to try first, start with Libby if you have a library card—it's a great way to explore books for free.

2. Download the App

Visit your device's app store (Apple App Store or Google Play Store) and search for the reading app you've chosen. Tap "Download" or "Install" to get it on your device.

3. Create an Account

Most apps will ask you to create an account or log in. You'll typically need to enter your email address and set a password. For Libby, you'll also need your library card number. Don't worry—it's a quick process, and you're almost ready to start reading!

4. Browse for Books

Open the app and explore the selection. Look for categories like "New Releases," "Top Picks," or "Free Books," or use the search bar to find a specific title or author. If you're using Libby, you can check out books just like at a physical library. For apps like Kindle or Apple Books, you may need to purchase the book before you can start reading.

5. Customize Your Reading Experience

When you open a book, you can adjust the settings to make reading more comfortable. You can increase the text size, change the background color, or switch to Dark Mode for easier nighttime reading. You can also choose between scrolling through the text or turning pages, whichever feels more natural to you.

Grandson's Tech Tip: If you're finding the text too small, go into the settings and increase the font size. It's like getting a large-print book, but without needing a special edition!

Navigating and Personalizing Your Reading

Flipping pages on a reading app is simple: swipe left or tap the right side of the screen to move forward, and swipe right or tap the left side to go back. Most apps will automatically save your place, so you don't need to worry about bookmarks.

Want to remember a special quote or section? Press and hold on the text to highlight it, or tap the bookmark icon to save the page. You can even add notes, just like jotting down a thought in the margin of a book.

The Joy of Digital Reading

Reading apps bring the joy of reading right to your fingertips. Whether you're enjoying an audiobook while cooking, flipping through a novel on your tablet, or borrowing a book from the library on Libby, there's something for everyone. You have complete control over your reading experience—choose what you want to read, when you want to read, and how you want to read it.

So go ahead and give it a try. Download a reading app, find a book you've been meaning to read, and start exploring. You're doing fantastic, and I'm right here cheering you on as you take each step in your digital reading journey.

Game Time: The Digital Grandson's Guide to Fun

Discover How to Play Your Favorite Games on Your Smartphone, Tablet, or Computer

Playing games has always been a fun way to pass the time, exercise your brain, and unwind. Thanks to technology, you can now enjoy a wide range of games directly on your smartphone, tablet, or computer—no more digging through the closet for board games or shuffling a deck of cards! In this chapter, I'll introduce you to some popular types of digital games and guide you through the basics of getting started. Whether you love puzzles, card games, or testing your knowledge with trivia, there's something for everyone. Let's dive in together!

Why Play Games on Your Device?

Playing games on your device is a wonderful way to keep your mind active, have fun, and even stay connected with loved ones. Unlike traditional board or card games that require setup, digital games are ready to play with just the tap of a button. You can play for a few minutes while waiting for the kettle to boil, or for an hour when you want to fully unwind—it's completely up to you.

Plus, many games can help sharpen skills like memory, problem-solving, and hand-eye coordination. Some even allow you to compete against friends or family members, whether they're in the next room or across the country. Let's explore some of the most popular games you might enjoy.

Popular Types of Digital Games

You'll find a wide variety of games available on your device. Here's a look at some of the most popular categories, each offering something unique:

1. Puzzle Games

Puzzle games are great for keeping your mind sharp. Whether you're solving a Sudoku, matching colorful candies in **Candy Crush**, or piecing together a digital jigsaw puzzle, these games let you go at your own pace. If you enjoy tackling challenges and feeling that sense of accomplishment, puzzle games might be just the thing for you.

Tip: Many puzzle games, like **Candy Crush**, are free to play but may offer in-app purchases for extra features. You can enjoy the game without spending money, so don't feel pressured to buy anything unless you want to.

2. Card and Board Games

If you love classics like **Solitaire**, **Bridge**, **Chess**, or **Scrabble**, you're in luck—these games are available as apps! You can play against the computer, a random opponent, or even invite a friend to join you online. It's a wonderful way to enjoy familiar games without needing to clear the dining room table.

Tip: Not sure about the rules? Many of these apps include helpful tutorials and guides to get you started, so you can brush up on your skills or learn a new game without feeling overwhelmed.

3. Trivia and Word Games

Love testing your knowledge or playing with words? Games like **Words with Friends** or **Trivia Crack** are perfect choices. You can play at your own pace and challenge friends and family, making it a great way to stay connected and maybe even learn a fun fact or two!

Fun Fact: Did you know? In **Words with Friends**, you can chat with your opponent directly in the game. It's a fun way to say hello or share a friendly note while you play.

4. Strategy and Simulation Games

Strategy games like **FarmVille** or **Township** let you build virtual towns or farms. These games are all about planning and decision-making, allowing you to watch your creation grow over time. They're great if you enjoy projects that require thought and patience, like gardening or cooking a slow-cooked meal.

Note: Many strategy games offer optional in-app purchases for faster progress, but there's no rush—take your time and enjoy watching your town or farm flourish.

5. Action and Adventure Games

If you're looking for something a bit more exciting, action games like **Angry Birds** or **Temple Run** provide a fun challenge. These games often involve quick thinking and fast reactions, making them a great option if you're in the mood for something fast-paced. Don't worry if it takes a few tries to get the hang of it—practice makes perfect!

Getting Started with Digital Games

Ready to play? All you need is a smartphone, tablet, or computer, an internet connection, and access to an app store for downloading games. Here's how to get started:

Choose a Game

The **App Store** (for Apple devices) and the **Google Play Store** (for Android devices) are like digital libraries filled with apps, including games of all kinds. Think of it like browsing the aisles of your favorite shop—you can look around, see what catches your eye, and pick what you'd like to try.

Browse and Download a Game

1. **Open the App Store**: On your device, find and tap the App Store (Apple) or Google Play Store (Android).

2. **Search for a Game**: Use the search bar to look for a specific game or browse by category, like "Puzzle Games" or "Card Games."

3. **Download**: Once you've found a game you like, tap **Download** or **Install**. Many games are free, but some may have a cost or offer extra features through **in-app purchases**.

Set Up Your Game

1. **Open the Game**: Once installed, go to your home screen and tap the game icon. Most games include a quick tutorial to show you the basics. Take your time and follow along—there's no rush!

2. **Create an Account (Optional)**: Some games might ask you to create an account. This helps save your progress and lets you play on different devices. It's usually optional, so you can skip this step if you prefer.

Tips for Enjoying Digital Games

1. **Take Breaks**: It's easy to get absorbed in a game, but remember to take breaks. Stretch, move around, and rest your eyes—especially if you've been playing for a while.

2. **Play with Friends**: Many games let you connect with friends and family, making it a fun way to stay in touch. Games like **Scrabble** or **Words with Friends** are great for a little friendly competition.

3. **Try New Games**: Don't be afraid to explore different types of games. You might discover a new favorite, whether it's a trivia challenge or a relaxing strategy game.

Embracing the Joy of Digital Games

Playing games on your device can be an enjoyable and rewarding way to spend your time. Whether you're solving a puzzle, competing in a word game, or tending to a virtual farm, there's always something new to discover. Remember, the goal is to have fun—there's no right or wrong way to play.

So go ahead, try a game that looks interesting. You're doing great, and I'm here cheering you on as you learn and enjoy new ways to stay entertained. Let's keep exploring together, one game, one challenge, and one victory at a time!

READING NEWS ONLINE

DIGITAL GRANDSON PRESS

Your Guide to Staying Informed: Exploring News Websites and Apps with Ease

Simple Steps to Access the Latest Headlines and Updates—Your Digital Grandson is Here to Help!

Staying informed has never been easier, thanks to news websites and apps. With just a few taps on your device, you can access the latest news, articles, and updates from around the world. In this chapter, we'll explore how to use these tools to stay up to date in a way that feels simple and enjoyable. Don't worry—if you get a little lost, I'm right here with you!

What Are News Websites and Apps?

Think of **news websites** as digital versions of your favorite newspapers. Instead of flipping through pages, you can scroll through articles, watch videos, and keep up with the latest events online. **News apps** work similarly, but they're designed specifically for smartphones and tablets, so you can check the news anytime, whether you're at home or on the go.

A quick way to remember: news websites are like a digital newspaper, and news apps are like having a pocket-sized update on everything happening around you. They cover topics like politics, sports, entertainment, and local events—there's something for everyone!

Getting Started with News Websites and Apps

Before we dive in, make sure you have a **smartphone, tablet, or computer** with an internet connection. Let's get started together!

Accessing News Websites

1. **Open Your Web Browser**:

   - Tap on your browser app (such as **Safari**, **Chrome**, or **Firefox**). Think of your browser as a window to the internet—it's your gateway to any website you want to visit.

2. **Search for a News Website**:

   - In the address bar, type in the name of a news website, like **CNN.com**, **BBC.com**, or **NYTimes.com**. If you're not sure where to start, simply type **"latest news"** in the search bar, and you'll see popular options.

3. **Explore the Homepage**:

   - Once you're on the website, you'll see the most recent news stories on the homepage. Scroll down to see different articles or click on categories like **World**, **Sports**, or **Entertainment** to find what interests you.

4. **Read an Article**:

   - To read a story, tap or click on the headline or picture.

This will open the full article. Simply scroll down to continue reading. Many websites also include related photos or videos that can help bring the story to life.

Pro Tip: If you find the text too small, try zooming in by spreading two fingers apart on the screen or using your browser's **Text Size** option. Your eyes will thank you!

Using News Apps

If you prefer a more streamlined experience, a news app might be the way to go. Here's how to get started:

1. **Download the News App**:

   - Open your device's **App Store** (for iPhones) or **Google Play Store** (for Android devices). Search for the news app you want, like **BBC News**, **CNN**, or **The New York Times**. Tap **Download** or **Install** to add it to your device.

   - If you have an iPhone, you might already have **Apple News** installed—give it a try!

2. **Sign Up or Log In**:

   - Some apps may ask you to create an account or log in. This step is optional but can help you customize your news feed. Remember, some apps may require a **subscription** to access all articles, so keep an eye out for any prompts about paywalls.

3. **Browse the Headlines**:

- When you open the app, you'll see the top headlines on the homepage. Tap any headline to read the full story. Feel free to take your time—there's no rush!

4. **Explore Categories**:

    - Most news apps have sections like **World News**, **Local News**, **Politics**, and **Health**. Tap the **Menu button** (it often looks like three horizontal lines, sometimes called a "hamburger icon"—no fries included, unfortunately!) and choose a category that interests you.

Pro Tip: Many apps have a **Save for Later** option if you come across an article you want to read but don't have time for right now. Look for a little bookmark or save icon.

Setting Up Notifications

Want to be notified when big news breaks? Here's how to set up alerts:

1. **Allow Notifications**:

    - When you first install a news app, it may ask if you'd like to enable notifications. Tap **Allow** if you want updates sent directly to your device. You can always change this later in your device's settings.

2. **Customize Notifications**:

    - Don't want to be overwhelmed with alerts? No problem! Go to the app's **Settings** section and adjust your preferences. You can choose to only receive notifications about certain topics, like **local news** or **weather alerts**.

Pro Tip: If you find notifications distracting, consider turning on **Do Not Disturb** mode on your device. This way, you can catch up on the news at a time that suits you.

Tips for Using News Websites and Apps

- **Bookmark Your Favorite Sites**:

  - If there's a news website you visit often, bookmark it in your browser for quick access. This way, you won't need to type in the address every time—just tap the bookmark.

- **Try Using Voice Commands**:

  - You can ask your voice assistant for help. Try saying, "Hey Siri, open BBC News," or "Okay Google, show me the latest headlines." It's like having a personal news butler!

- **Adjust Text Size and Enable Dark Mode**:

  - If the text feels too small, look for a **Text Size** option in the app's settings. Many apps also have a **Dark Mode** feature, which can be easier on your eyes, especially at night.

- **Explore Audio and Video Options**:

  - Many apps offer **podcasts** or **live video updates**. It's a great way to stay informed if you'd prefer listening or watching instead of reading.

Staying Informed

Using news websites and apps is a wonderful way to feel connected to the world, whether you're reading the latest headlines, discovering a new favorite article, or watching video updates. You're already taking great steps by exploring these tools, and I'm here to cheer you on!

So go ahead, open that news app, find an interesting story, and enjoy learning about what's happening in the world today. Remember, you've got this, and I'm right here if you need a helping hand. Together, we'll make sure staying informed is easy and enjoyable.

Staying Informed: How to Find Trustworthy News in a Digital World

Simple Tips for Spotting Reliable Sources and Avoiding Misinformation—Your Digital Grandson is Here to Guide You!

With so much information available online, it's easy to feel overwhelmed. (It seems like anyone can post anything these days, true or not!) But don't worry—I'm here to help you figure out how to find news you can trust. In this chapter, we'll walk through some simple ways to spot reliable sources and avoid falling for misinformation. Together, we'll build your confidence in navigating the world of news.

What Makes a News Source Trustworthy?

A trustworthy news source gives you accurate, well-researched information and presents it fairly. These sources follow ethical guidelines, employ professional journalists, and provide evidence to back up their stories. Here's what to look for:

- **Established Reputation**: Trusted news sources are often well-known organizations that have been around for many years. They've built a reputation for reliable reporting.

- **Multiple Sources**: Credible news outlets don't rely on a single source—they check facts and often cite multiple experts or studies. It's like getting a second opinion from a trusted friend.

- **Balanced Reporting**: Good news sources present different sides of an issue. They don't try to sensationalize stories or stir up fear—they stick to the facts.

- **Transparent Corrections**: Mistakes happen to everyone. The best news outlets own up to errors and issue corrections, showing they care about getting it right.

How to Evaluate Online News Sources

If you come across a news story online, take a moment to ask yourself a few key questions before believing it right away. Here's how we can check for credibility together:

1. **Who Published It?**

   - Look at the author and the organization behind the story. Are they well-known? Do they have a history of accurate reporting? If you don't recognize the name, a quick search can help you learn more about them.

2. **Is There Evidence?**

   - Check if the article includes evidence to support its claims. Look for links to original sources, interviews with experts, or references to research. If it feels like the story is missing details, it might not be as reliable.

3. **Watch for Bias**:

    - A good news story shares multiple viewpoints. If the article seems one-sided or pushes a specific agenda, it's worth being cautious. Remember, news should help inform you, not sway your opinion.

4. **Look for Sensational Language**:

    - Reliable news uses clear, straightforward language. Be wary of headlines that use dramatic words to grab your attention—they're often more interested in clicks than in the truth.

Pro Tip: If something sounds too shocking or unbelievable, it's a good idea to double-check it with another trusted source. Just like you'd get a second opinion at the doctor, it's smart to verify surprising news stories.

Tips for Finding Reliable News Sources

Here are a few simple strategies to help you find trustworthy news:

- **Stick to Well-Known Outlets**: Stick to sites that have long histories of balanced reporting. They may not be perfect, but they have a strong track record.

- **Cross-Check Information**: If you see a news story that seems surprising or upsetting, take a moment to look it up on another reliable news site. If multiple credible sources are reporting the same story, it's more likely to be true.

- **Use Fact-Checking Websites**: Websites like **Snopes**, **FactCheck.org**, and **PolitiFact** specialize in debunking false claims. If you're ever unsure about a story, these sites can help set the record straight.

- **Be Cautious with Social Media**: News spreads quickly on social media, but it's not always accurate. Before believing or sharing a story, take a moment to verify it with a reputable news outlet. It's worth the extra effort to avoid spreading misinformation.

Tools for Checking News Credibility

Let's go over a few handy tools you can use to assess the reliability of a news source:

1. **Check the Editorial Board**:

    - Reputable news organizations have an editorial board made up of experienced journalists who oversee the content. If you can see who's in charge and learn about their credentials, it's a good sign that the publication follows high standards.

2. **Look for Author Information**:

    - Trustworthy articles usually include the author's name and background. If an article doesn't list who wrote it or their qualifications, consider that a red flag.

3. **Check the Date**:

    - Always look at the publication date. Sometimes old news

stories resurface and spread as if they were new, which can be confusing.

4. **Supporting Evidence**:

    - Credible articles often link to original sources, like official statements or research papers. If a story makes bold claims without any supporting evidence, it's best to proceed with caution.

Pro Tip: If you find the text hard to read, most news websites and apps offer options to increase the text size or switch to **Dark Mode**, which can be easier on your eyes.

Finding Credible Information

Knowing how to evaluate the news you read is an important part of staying informed and making good decisions. It's normal to feel unsure at first, but remember: you're already taking great steps by learning these skills. Questioning what you read isn't a sign of doubt—it's a sign of a smart, critical thinker!

Pro Tip: It's okay to take your time. If you come across a story that doesn't seem quite right, there's no rush to share it or form an opinion. Take a moment, do a little digging, and feel confident in your ability to make an informed choice.

Stay Curious and Confident

You've got all the tools you need to find credible news sources and avoid falling for misinformation. Keep exploring different news websites, double-check surprising stories, and use the fact-checking tools we discussed. Remember, it's not about knowing everything right away—it's about taking it step by step and building your confidence.

So go ahead and dive into the world of news with a critical eye, knowing that I'm here to support you every step of the way. You're doing great, and together we'll keep you informed and empowered. Let's keep learning and discovering the facts—one story at a time.

Smart Homes

Digital Grandson Press

A Cozy Guide to Smart Homes: Making Life Easier, One Device at a Time

Simple, Step-by-Step Tips for Adding Comfort and Convenience to Your Home—Your Digital Grandson is Here to Help!

Imagine relaxing in your favorite chair and being able to turn off the lights, adjust the thermostat, or even lock the doors—all without getting up. That's the magic of a smart home! In this chapter, we'll explore what smart home devices are, how they work, and how they can make your life more comfortable and enjoyable. Don't worry if this feels new or unfamiliar—I'm here to guide you every step of the way.

What is a "Smart Home"?

A **smart home** is simply a home that has devices you can control using your smartphone, tablet, or even your voice. These devices can help with everyday tasks like turning on the lights, adjusting the temperature, or playing your favorite music. Think of it like having a helpful assistant around the house—someone who listens to your commands and never forgets to follow through.

Smart home devices can include **smart speakers** (like Alexa or Google Home), **smart thermostats**, **smart lights**, and even **smart plugs**, which let you control regular appliances remotely. The best part is that you don't need to transform your entire home overnight. You can start with just one or two devices and add more as you gain confidence and get comfortable.

Why Consider Smart Home Devices?

Smart home technology isn't just about fancy gadgets—it's about making life a little easier and adding comfort to your daily routine. Here's how smart home devices can help:

- **Convenience**: Imagine turning off the lights from bed with a simple voice command. No more getting up in the dark and searching for a switch. It's like having your own personal helper right at your side.

- **Energy Savings**: Smart thermostats can help save on energy costs by learning your preferences and automatically adjusting the temperature. It's like having a thermostat that knows you like it warm in the morning and cool at night.

- **Safety and Security**: With smart locks and security cameras, you can keep an eye on your home, even when you're away. It's a great way to have peace of mind—just open the app and check that everything is as it should be.

- **Entertainment**: Smart speakers can play music, tell jokes, and even answer your questions. It's a fun way to enjoy your favorite tunes or get quick updates, all hands-free.

Getting to Know Popular Smart Home Devices

Let's take a closer look at some of the most common smart home devices you might want to start with.

Smart Speakers (e.g., Amazon Echo, Google Home)

What They Do: Smart speakers can play music, answer questions, set reminders, and control other smart devices in your home.

How They Help: Picture yourself making coffee in the morning and asking, "What's the weather today?" Your smart speaker will give you an instant answer—no need to grab your phone or turn on the TV. It's like having a friendly voice assistant who's always ready to help.

Smart Lights (e.g., Philips Hue, LIFX)

What They Do: Smart lights can be turned on and off using an app or a simple voice command. You can also dim them or change the color to set the mood.

How They Help: Instead of fumbling for a light switch in the dark, just say, "Alexa, turn on the living room lights." You can even schedule them to turn on at specific times, so your home feels welcoming when you walk in.

Smart Thermostats (e.g., Nest, Ecobee)

What They Do: A smart thermostat learns your temperature preferences and automatically adjusts the settings to keep you comfortable.

How It Works: Imagine it's a chilly morning, and your thermostat has already warmed up the house before you even get out of bed. It's like having your own personal butler, but just for temperature control!

Smart Plugs

What They Do: Smart plugs turn regular appliances into smart ones. Just plug in a lamp or a fan, and you can now control it from your phone.

How They Help: If you're out and can't remember whether you turned off the living room lamp, you can check and turn it off using the app. It's a simple way to save energy and give yourself peace of mind.

Smart Locks (e.g., August, Schlage)

What They Do: Smart locks let you lock and unlock your door using your phone. You can also give temporary access to others without needing a spare key.

How They Help: No more hiding keys under the doormat! If a friend needs to stop by, you can easily grant them access through the app. Plus, you can double-check that the door is locked, even if you're already tucked in bed.

Tips for Using Smart Home Devices

- **Start Small**: You don't need to make your entire home "smart" right away. Start with one or two devices that simplify your life, like a smart speaker or a few smart lights. Once you get comfortable, you can explore adding more.

- **Use Voice Commands**: Talking to your devices might feel strange at first, but it can quickly become second nature. The smart speaker is often the hub of a smart home, making it easy to control everything with a simple voice command. Try saying, "Turn off the lights," or "Play my favorite music." It's like having your own personal assistant—who's always polite and never complains!

- **Set Routines**: Many smart devices let you create routines, which are a series of actions triggered by a single command. For example, you could set up a "Good Night" routine that turns off the lights, locks the doors, and lowers the thermostat—all with one simple phrase.

Pro Tip: If you're ever unsure about how to use a device, don't hesitate to ask your smart speaker for help. Just say, "How do I use smart lights?" and it can guide you through the process.

The Comfort of a Smart Home

Smart home devices are designed to make life easier and more enjoyable. Whether you're turning off the lights from bed, adjusting the temperature without getting up, or asking your smart speaker to tell you a joke, these little helpers can add a lot of comfort and fun to your daily routine.

Don't be afraid to try out a smart speaker or a set of smart lights—you might be surprised at how quickly you get used to the convenience. And remember, I'm right here with you, cheering you on as you explore new ways to make your home even cozier.

You're doing fantastic! Let's continue discovering how technology can make your life a little easier, one step at a time.

Getting Started with Smart Speakers: Your Friendly Guide to Making Your Home Smarter

Simple, Step-by-Step Help from Your Digital Grandson

Setting up a smart speaker is one of the easiest and most rewarding ways to begin building a smart home. A smart speaker, such as an Amazon Echo (with Alexa) or Google Nest (with Google Assistant), can help you control everything from music to lights—all with your voice. It's like having a helpful assistant right there in your living room, ready to lend a hand whenever you need it. In this chapter, we'll guide you through the setup process so you can start enjoying all the benefits right away. Don't worry if this feels new or a bit intimidating; I'm here with you every step of the way, just like a patient grandchild showing you the ropes.

What You Will Need

To set up your smart speaker, here's what you'll need:

1. **A Smart Speaker:** Choose one that fits your needs. Popular options include the Amazon Echo (Alexa) and Google Nest (Google Assistant).

2. **A Smartphone or Tablet:** This is how you'll set up and control your speaker using its app.

3. **Wi-Fi Connection:** Your smart speaker will need internet access to respond to your commands.

Step-by-Step Guide for Setting Up Your Smart Speaker

Step 1: Unbox and Plug In

Unbox your new smart speaker and plug it into a power outlet. You'll see a light turn on—that's the first sign it's waking up and ready to go! Place it in a convenient spot, like your kitchen or living room, where you can easily talk to it and hear its responses. It's okay to move it later if you find a better spot.

Step 2: Download the App

Now, grab your smartphone or tablet and download the app for your smart speaker:

- For Amazon Echo, download the **Amazon Alexa app**.

- For Google Nest, download the **Google Home app**.

Once you've got the app installed, open it up. It's like a little guidebook that will walk you through the next steps. Don't worry—I'll still be here if you get stuck.

Step 3: Connect to Wi-Fi

Your smart speaker needs to connect to your Wi-Fi to work properly. The app will guide you through this part. It might even fill in your Wi-Fi details automatically if your phone is already connected. If not, just have your Wi-Fi password handy.

Step 4: Test a Simple Command

Now comes the fun part—talking to your smart speaker! Try saying:

- "Hey Google, what's the weather today?"
- "Alexa, play some music."

Don't worry if you get tongue-tied at first. It's normal to feel a little silly talking to a speaker, but you'll get used to it quickly.

Step 5: Personalize Your Preferences

The app may ask if you want to set up some preferences, like linking your music services (Spotify, Amazon Music) or creating voice profiles for different family members. You can skip these for now if you prefer, but they're easy to set up later once you're more comfortable.

Common Features to Try

Your smart speaker can do a lot of things to make your life easier. Here are a few ideas to get you started:

- **Play Music:** Say, "Alexa, play some jazz" or "Hey Google, play my favorite songs." Your speaker will play music from services like Spotify, Amazon Music, or YouTube Music.

- **Set Reminders and Alarms:** Need a reminder? Just say, "Alexa, remind me to take my pills at 3 PM," or "Hey Google, set an alarm for 8 AM."

- **Control Smart Home Devices:** If you have smart lights or plugs, you can control them with your voice. Try, "Hey Google, turn off the kitchen lights," or "Alexa, turn on the fan."

Troubleshooting Common Problems

Even though setting up your smart speaker is usually simple, sometimes things don't go as planned. Here's how to handle a few common issues:

- **Speaker Not Responding:** Check that it's plugged in and the light is on. If it's still not working, try unplugging it for a few seconds and then plugging it back in.

- **Wi-Fi Connection Issues:** Make sure you've entered the correct Wi-Fi password. If your speaker keeps disconnecting, try moving it closer to your router. It can also help to connect it to the 2.4 GHz Wi-Fi network instead of the 5 GHz one.

- **Voice Commands Not Recognized:** Speak slowly and clearly. If your speaker still doesn't understand, try adjusting the app's language or region settings to better match your voice.

- **No Sound or Music:** Make sure the volume isn't muted. You can say, "Alexa, increase the volume," or use the volume buttons on the speaker.

Making the Most of Your Smart Speaker

Here are some tips to help you get the most out of your new device:

- **Get Comfortable with Voice Commands:** It might feel a bit strange at first, but once you get the hang of it, you'll see how convenient it is. It's like having a friendly assistant who never needs a break!

- **Explore the App:** The app is like your speaker's instruction manual. Take a few minutes to browse through it and see what else your smart speaker can do.

- **Set Up Routines:** Many smart speakers let you create routines that do multiple things at once. For example, saying "Good morning" can turn on your lights, give you the weather, and start playing your favorite news podcast.

Final Thoughts

Congratulations! You've set up your smart speaker and taken your first step toward a smarter home. It's okay if you don't feel like an expert yet—every time you use it, you'll learn something new. Remember, I'm here to guide you whenever you need help, just like I would if I were right there with you.

So go ahead—ask it a question, play some music, or set a reminder. You're doing fantastic, and I can't wait for you to discover all the ways your smart speaker can make your life a little easier and a lot more fun.

SHOPPING ONLINE

DIGITAL GRANDSON PRESS

Shopping from Home: A Beginner's Guide to Online Shopping

How to Find What You Need, Make Safe Purchases, and Enjoy the Convenience of Shopping Online

Online shopping has made it easier than ever to get what you need without leaving your house. Whether you're looking for a cozy sweater, groceries for the week, or a special gift for a loved one, you can find it all with just a few clicks. In this chapter, we'll go through the basics of online shopping together, explain how it works, and help you feel confident making your first purchase. Don't worry if this feels new—I'll guide you every step of the way.

What Is Online Shopping?

Think of online shopping as browsing through a big, virtual catalog, but with way more options than any store you've ever visited. Instead of driving to a physical shop, you use your computer, smartphone, or tablet to search for items, compare prices, and make purchases. It's like having the entire mall right at your fingertips, minus the crowds and parking hassle!

Some of the most popular online stores include Amazon, Walmart, Target, and even smaller specialty shops you might not find in your local area. You can shop from big-name retailers or support independent sellers—all from the comfort of your own home. So grab a cup of tea, get comfortable, and let's dive in.

Why Should You Shop Online?

If you're wondering whether online shopping is for you, here are some great reasons to give it a try:

1. Convenience

You can shop any time, day or night, without worrying about store hours or weather conditions. Whether you're at home in your favorite chair or visiting family, all you need is an internet connection. And the best part? You can do it all in your pajamas—no judgment here! Plus, many stores make returns simple, so you don't have to worry if something isn't quite right.

2. Variety

Online stores often carry a wider range of products than you'd find in a physical shop. Looking for a specific size, color, or brand? You can easily compare options without walking down multiple aisles. It's like being able to peek into every store in the mall without moving an inch.

3. Home Delivery

Once you've placed your order, the items will be delivered right to your door. Many retailers even offer free shipping or express delivery if you need something quickly. It's like having your own personal delivery service. Just keep an eye out for packages—sometimes they arrive before you've even had time to check your email!

Popular Shopping Sites

There are plenty of great places to shop online, each offering something a little different. Here's a quick guide to some of the most popular options and what they're best for:

- **Amazon:** Amazon is like the giant warehouse of the internet. You can find almost anything here, from electronics and clothing to household items. If you sign up for Amazon Prime, you can enjoy fast, often free shipping. It's a great choice if you like getting things quickly.

- **Walmart:** Walmart offers a wide selection of groceries, clothing, electronics, and home essentials. You can shop online for delivery or order for in-store pick-up if you prefer. Their prices are budget-friendly, making it a good option for everyday items.

- **Target:** Target is known for its stylish and affordable products, including clothing, home decor, and groceries. They often have exclusive collections that you won't find anywhere else. You can choose home delivery or pick-up at a local store.

- **eBay:** eBay is great if you're looking for unique or second-hand items. You can bid on products in an auction or buy them right away. It's a bit like a digital garage sale—you never know what treasures you might find.

- **Etsy:** If you love handmade or vintage items, Etsy is the place to go. It's filled with products made by small business owners and artisans. Whether you're looking for a special gift or something unique for your home, Etsy has plenty of one-of-a-kind options.

- **Best Buy:** Best Buy specializes in electronics and tech gadgets. Need a new phone, laptop, or kitchen appliance? Best Buy offers a wide selection and has plenty of customer reviews to help you choose the right product.

- **Wayfair:** Looking to spruce up your home? Wayfair offers a huge variety of furniture and home decor items, often at great prices. It's perfect for finding everything from a new sofa to a decorative rug.

- **Instacart:** If grocery shopping is on your list, Instacart lets you order from local stores and have the items delivered the same day. It's especially handy if you need fresh produce or pantry staples in a hurry.

- **Zappos:** Zappos is a fantastic site for shoes and accessories. They have an easy returns policy, so you can order multiple sizes and send back what doesn't fit, hassle-free.

- **Chewy:** Have a furry friend? Chewy is your go-to for pet supplies. They offer everything from pet food to toys, with an option for automatic deliveries so you never run out of treats.

Tips for Safe Online Shopping

I know security might be a concern, so here are a few quick tips to help you feel more at ease:

- **Shop on Trusted Websites:** Look for well-known retailers or check for a padlock icon next to the website's address—that means the site is secure.

- **Use Secure Payment Methods:** Pay with a credit card or a secure payment service like PayPal, which offers buyer protection in case something goes wrong.

- **Keep an Eye Out for Scams:** Be cautious of deals that seem too good to be true, and never share your personal information with a site you don't trust. If something doesn't feel right, take a step back and ask for help—I'm here if you need me!

Final Thoughts

Online shopping can open up a world of possibilities, from finding great deals to discovering unique items that you won't find in local stores. And the best part? You can do it all without having to drive, park, or stand in line. Whether you're shopping for essentials or treating yourself, online shopping makes the whole process simple and enjoyable.

Ready to give it a try? Find something you've been wanting, add it to your cart, and enjoy the convenience of having it delivered right to your door. You've got this, and I'm here if you need any help along the way. Together, we'll make sure your online shopping experience is smooth, safe, and maybe even a little bit fun.

Starting with Online Shopping

Your Step-by-Step Guide

Welcome! If you've ever wondered about online shopping but felt unsure where to start, you're in the right place. Let's go through it step by step together. It's a lot like shopping at your favorite store—just from the comfort of your own home. And don't worry, I'll be right here with you the whole way. Let's get started!

What You'll Need Before You Begin

Before we dive in, here are a few things you'll need:

1. **A Device**: You can use a smartphone, tablet, or computer—whichever feels most comfortable for you. It's like choosing which cookbook to grab from the shelf; any of them will work!

2. **Internet Connection**: This is your gateway to online stores, like a bridge connecting you to the world of products. Make sure your device is connected to Wi-Fi or a mobile network.

3. **An Account (Optional but Helpful)**: Many online stores will ask you to create an account using your name, email

address, and a password. This can make future purchases faster and help track your orders. But don't worry—you can often shop as a guest if you prefer to keep it simple.

4. **A Payment Method**: To pay for your items, you can use a credit card, debit card, PayPal, or even digital wallets like Apple Pay or Google Pay. We'll go over these in more detail a bit later, so there's no need to memorize anything yet.

Step 1: Choose Where to Shop

Think of this step like deciding which store to visit at the mall. You can head straight to a well-known online store, like Amazon, Walmart, or Target, or use a search engine like Google to find a specific item. If you're using a mobile device, you can also download the store's app for a smoother experience.

When you're ready, type the store's web address into your browser's search bar (e.g., www.amazon.com), or tap on the app icon if you've installed it. If you're ever unsure, feel free to pause and take your time. We're not in a rush!

Step 2: Browse or Search for Items

Browsing online is a lot like wandering the aisles at your favorite store, but without the heavy shopping cart. You can use the **search bar** at the top of the page to look for something specific, like "blue sweater" or "wireless headphones." Or, you can explore categories like clothing, electronics, or home goods.

Tip: Use the store's filters to narrow down your options by price, brand, or customer ratings. It's like having a personal shopper who helps you find exactly what you need without the extra legwork.

Step 3: Add Items to Your Cart

When you find something you like, click **Add to Cart**. This is just like placing an item into your grocery cart—you can keep adding things until you're ready to check out.

Before You Click Add: Take a moment to click on the item for more details. Check the product description, read customer reviews, and look at the Q&A section to ensure it's exactly what you want. If you change your mind later, no problem! Just go to your cart (usually a shopping cart icon at the top of the page) and click **Remove** next to the item.

Step 4: Review Your Cart and Proceed to Checkout

Now that you've added everything you want, it's time to take a look at your cart. Click the cart icon to review your items. Double-check the sizes, quantities, and colors—it's better to catch any mistakes now rather than later.

Helpful Tip: If you have a coupon or promo code, this is the time to enter it. Look for a box that says "Enter Promo Code" at checkout. It's like finding a surprise discount at the register!

When you're ready, click **Proceed to Checkout**.

Step 5: Enter Your Shipping Details

You'll need to provide your address so the store knows where to send your order. Many stores will ask if you'd like to save this address for future purchases. It's your choice—saving it can make checkout faster next time, but you can always enter it manually if you prefer.

Choose a Shipping Option: Most stores offer several choices, such as standard (slower but cheaper), express, or two-day shipping. Pick the one that suits your needs.

Step 6: Choose a Payment Method

Here comes the part where you pay for your items. You can enter your credit or debit card information, or use a digital payment service like PayPal, Apple Pay, or Google Pay. These options are like having a digital wallet—safe, secure, and convenient.

Review Your Payment Details: Double-check your card number, expiration date, and billing address. It's a quick step that can save you from any hiccups.

Step 7: Place Your Order

Take one last look at your order summary. Check that your items, shipping address, and payment information are all correct. If everything looks good, click **Place Order** or **Buy Now**. Congratulations—you've done it!

You should receive a confirmation email shortly after placing your order. It will include all the details of your purchase, plus an order number for tracking.

Tracking Your Order

Most stores allow you to track your order once it's shipped. Look for a **Track Order** link in your confirmation email or visit your account on the store's website. It's like following your package on its journey to your front door!

How to Return an Item: No Stress, I Promise

Sometimes things don't work out, and that's okay. Here's a quick guide to returning an item:

1. **Log In** to the website or app where you made your purchase.

2. Go to **Your Orders** and find the item you want to return.

3. Click on **Return or Replace Items**, then select a reason for the return (e.g., didn't fit, changed my mind).

4. Choose a **Return Method**, such as mailing it back or dropping it off at a store.

5. **Print the Return Label** (if needed), then pack the item securely.

6. Send it back and track your return. You'll receive an update when the store processes your refund.

Just take it one step at a time. If you need help, I'm right here!

Popular Ways to Pay Online

- **PayPal**: Think of this as your online wallet—quick and secure.

- **Apple Pay**: If you have an iPhone or iPad, Apple Pay lets you check out with just a tap.

- **Google Pay**: Similar to Apple Pay, but for Android devices. It's like paying with a digital card in your phone's pocket.

These payment options are safe, convenient, and often faster than typing in your card details.

Tips for Safe Online Shopping

1. **Stick to Trusted Websites** like Amazon, Target, or Walmart.

2. Look for **"https://"** in the web address—the "s" stands for secure.

3. Use a **strong password** for your accounts.

4. **Trust your gut**: If a deal looks too good to be true, it probably is.

Final Thoughts: You've Got This!

Online shopping might seem tricky at first, but it gets easier each time you try it. Remember, it's okay to take your time and ask questions if you're unsure. I'm here to help you feel confident and enjoy the experience. Happy shopping, and don't hesitate to reach out if you need a hand—I'm just a click away!

USING NAVIGATION APPS

DIGITAL GRANDSON PRESS

Navigating the World with GPS

Your Friendly Guide to Getting Around

Have you ever wished you didn't have to fumble with a paper map or ask someone for directions? That's where GPS comes in! In this chapter, we'll explore what GPS is, how it works, and how you can use it to find your way, whether you're heading to a new restaurant or visiting a friend in another city. I'll also introduce you to some of the most popular GPS apps that can make navigating easier than ever. Ready? Let's dive in!

What Does GPS Mean?

GPS stands for **Global Positioning System**. Think of it as a smart digital map that always knows exactly where you are. Instead of needing to ask for directions or figure out a route yourself, GPS guides you in real time, like having a helpful friend sitting beside you who never gets lost.

How Does GPS Work?

Imagine a group of friendly satellites high up in the sky, watching over us like a team of guides. These satellites send signals down to your device—whether it's your smartphone, tablet, or car navigation system. Your device picks up these signals and uses them to figure out your precise location. The best part? GPS updates in real time, so if you make a wrong turn, it quickly adjusts and gets you back on track. It's like having a co-pilot who always knows the way, even if you take an unexpected detour.

Most Common GPS Apps

There are many GPS apps out there, but let me introduce you to three of the most popular ones. Each has its own unique features, so you can pick the one that suits you best.

1. **Google Maps**
   Google Maps is like the go-to guide for getting around. It works on both Android and iOS devices, so whether you have an iPhone or a Samsung tablet, you're covered. With Google Maps, you can get directions for driving, walking, biking, or even using public transportation. It also gives you real-time traffic updates and shows you points of interest along the way, like nearby coffee shops or gas stations. It's like having a local tour guide who knows all the best spots!

2. **Apple Maps**
   If you're using an iPhone or iPad, you already have Apple Maps built in. It's super easy to use and provides turn-by-turn directions with a clear voice to guide you. Apple Maps also gives traffic updates and shows you nearby businesses, so you'll know if there's a coffee shop just around the corner. It's like having a friendly navigator who always has your back, even when you're exploring new places.

3. **Waze**
   Waze is the social butterfly of GPS apps. It's powered by drivers just like you, who share updates about road conditions, accidents, and even speed traps in real time. If you live in a busy city and want to avoid getting stuck in traffic, Waze can be a lifesaver. It's like having a whole community of drivers looking out for you and helping you find the fastest route.

How to Use GPS for Your Next Trip

Using a GPS app is as simple as typing in your destination and letting it do the work. Here's a quick guide to get you started:

1. **Open the App**: Tap on the GPS app of your choice—Google Maps, Apple Maps, or Waze.

2. **Enter Your Destination**: Type in where you want to go, like "Joe's Coffee Shop" or "123 Main Street."

3. **Choose Your Route**: The app will suggest a few different routes, showing you the estimated travel time for each. Pick the one that looks best to you.

4. **Start Navigation**: Tap the button that says **Start** or **Go**, and the app will begin giving you step-by-step directions. It's like having a guide who tells you exactly when to turn and where to go.

5. **Follow Along**: As you drive or walk, keep an eye on the screen or listen to the voice directions. If you miss a turn, don't worry—the app will quickly update and show you a

new route. It's okay to make mistakes; GPS is there to help you, not judge you!

Tips for Using GPS Like a Pro

1. **Double-Check the Destination**: Make sure you've entered the correct address before you start. It's easy to accidentally type in "123 Elm Street" instead of "123 Elm Avenue."

2. **Look at the Route Overview**: Before you head out, take a quick look at the route. It's like glancing at the map before you start driving—just to get a sense of where you're going.

3. **Adjust Your Volume**: If you're using voice directions, make sure the volume on your device is turned up enough so you can hear it clearly.

4. **Use Traffic Updates**: Apps like Google Maps and Waze will show you traffic conditions. If there's a big red line on your route, it means traffic is heavy—consider taking an alternate route if possible.

5. **Stay Safe**: If you're driving, try to use voice directions and keep your eyes on the road. If you need to look at the map, pull over safely first.

Final Thoughts: Let GPS Be Your Guide

GPS has made getting around easier and less stressful, especially if you're visiting a new place or running errands in an unfamiliar part of town. No more feeling lost or struggling with paper maps—just open your app, type in your destination, and let GPS do the rest. Remember, it's okay if it feels a bit tricky at first. With a little practice, you'll be navigating like a pro in no time. And if you ever feel unsure, just think of me as your personal tech support, ready to help whenever you need it. You've got this!

Using GPS

Your Step-by-Step Guide

Now that you've learned a bit about how GPS works, let's dive into how to use it step by step. Whether you're planning a big road trip or simply looking for a new coffee shop in town, GPS can make it easy to get there. Think of it as having a modern-day navigator — without the need to unfold a giant paper map!

Getting Started with Your GPS App

1. **Open Your GPS App**

   - Start by opening your GPS application. The most popular choices are Google Maps, Apple Maps, and Waze. To find the app, look for its icon on your smartphone or tablet's home screen and give it a tap.

   - **Tip:** If you're using a built-in navigation system in your car, this guide will still be helpful — the basics are quite similar.

2. **Enter Your Destination**

   - Once the app opens, you'll see a search bar at the top.

Tap on it and type in where you'd like to go. This could be a street address, a business name (like "Starbucks"), or even a well-known landmark, such as "Central Park."

- **Celebrating Wins:** Great job entering your destination! You're well on your way.

3. **Choose Your Route**

- After entering your destination, the app will suggest a few routes. You might see options like the fastest route, the shortest distance, or a route that avoids toll roads. Take a moment to review your choices and tap on the one that suits you best.

- **Note:** Sometimes, the app may default to the fastest route without showing other options. If you'd like to avoid tolls or highways, check the settings or preferences for "Route Options."

4. **Start Navigation**

- To begin your journey, simply tap the "Start" button. The app will then provide turn-by-turn directions, both visually on your screen and through voice prompts.

- **Safety Tip:** It's best to use a phone mount or dashboard holder while driving so you can keep your focus on the road. Let the voice directions guide you instead of glancing at the screen.

5. **Follow Voice Directions**

- Your GPS will say things like, "In 500 feet, turn left." Following the voice directions helps you keep your eyes on the road and makes for a safer driving experience. If you prefer, you can adjust the volume or connect your phone to your car's audio system.

6. **Re-routing When Needed**

- Missed a turn? No worries — it happens to the best of us! Your GPS app will automatically recalculate your route and give you new directions. Just follow the updated instructions, and you'll still reach your destination.

- **A Light Laugh:** Consider it a chance to take the scenic route!

Tips for Using GPS Effectively

1. **Check Traffic Conditions**

- Many GPS apps, like Google Maps and Waze, provide real-time traffic updates. Look for color-coded lines: green for smooth sailing, orange for moderate traffic, and red for heavy congestion. Use this information to choose the best route and avoid unexpected delays.

2. **Save Your Favorite Places**

- Save frequently visited locations, such as "Home" or "Work," so you don't have to type them in each time. In most apps, you'll find this feature under "Favorites" or "Saved Places."

3. **Use Offline Maps for Peace of Mind**

    - If you're heading to an area with spotty internet, download offline maps in advance. This way, you'll still have directions even if your connection drops. Offline maps won't update with real-time traffic, but they're great for navigating in a pinch.

4. **Zoom In and Out on the Map**

    - To get a closer look at the map, use your fingers to pinch the screen. This helps you see nearby landmarks or get a better sense of where you're headed. You can also use on-screen buttons if you find that easier.

5. **Follow Safety Guidelines**

    - Keep your phone on a dashboard holder, use voice directions, and avoid interacting with the app directly while driving. Remember, it's better to pull over safely if you need to make adjustments.

Troubleshooting Common GPS Issues

Even the best technology can have hiccups. Here's how to solve some common problems:

1. **GPS Signal Not Found**

    - If your GPS app says it can't find a signal, make sure you're in an open area without tall buildings or dense trees. You can also try restarting your device or switching in and out of airplane mode to reset the connection.

2. **Incorrect Location**

    - If your GPS is showing the wrong location, check that Location Services are enabled on your device. Go to your settings, find "Location Services," and ensure they're turned on. You might also need to update the app for the most accurate data.

    - **Pro Tip:** If you're prompted to "calibrate" your device, try moving it in a figure-eight motion. It's like giving your phone a little shake to help it get back on track!

3. **App Not Responding**

    - If the app freezes, close it and reopen. If that doesn't work, restart your device or check for updates on the App Store or Google Play. Clearing the app's cache (on Android) or freeing up storage space can also help.

4. **Slow Navigation Updates**

    - Slow updates could be due to a weak internet connection. Try switching between Wi-Fi and cellular data. Also, close any unnecessary apps running in the background to improve GPS performance.

5. **Voice Directions Not Working**

    - If you're not hearing voice directions, first check your device's volume. Make sure it's not muted. You may also need to go into the GPS app's settings and ensure voice guidance is enabled. If your phone is connected to a Bluetooth device, like your car's audio system, make sure the audio output is set correctly.

Battery-Saving Tips

GPS apps can drain your battery, especially during long trips. Here's how to conserve power:

- Reduce your screen brightness.

- Turn off Wi-Fi and Bluetooth if you don't need them.

- Close any apps you're not using.

- If you're driving, use a car charger to keep your phone powered up.

Final Thoughts: You've Got This!

Using GPS makes travel easier and more fun. There's no need to worry about getting lost or dealing with paper maps anymore. Whether you're exploring a new city, visiting a friend, or running errands, GPS is your helpful guide. And if you make a wrong turn? No big deal — it's just part of the adventure.

Go ahead and type in your next destination. You're doing great, and we're here to support you as you confidently explore the world. Remember, technology is here to help, and with every trip, you're getting more comfortable and confident. Safe travels, and happy exploring!

AI Tools

DIGITAL GRANDSON PRESS

AI Demystified: Your Guide to Understanding and Using Artificial Intelligence

A Friendly Introduction for Beginners and Curious Learners

Welcome to the World of Artificial Intelligence (AI)

Welcome to the exciting world of Artificial Intelligence (AI)! Now, before you start picturing robots taking over the world or your coffee maker starting a revolution, let me assure you: AI isn't as intimidating as it sounds. In fact, AI is already a part of our everyday lives, quietly working behind the scenes to make things a little easier for us. From helping you find the best route to a new restaurant to assisting me with writing this very guide, AI is here to lend a hand — not take over.

Let's explore what AI really is, how it works, and how you can use it to simplify your daily tasks. And don't worry if it feels like a lot to take in at first; we'll go through it step by step, just like I'd explain it to my own grandparents.

What Exactly Is AI?

Artificial intelligence, or AI, is simply a type of technology that can make decisions and learn new things — kind of like a smart assistant. Imagine you're asking your grandchild a question, and they give you a quick answer. AI is similar, but instead of relying on years of school and experience, it relies on large amounts of data and clever computer programs. It's like a digital helper that's great at finding information, answering questions, and even learning what you like.

In short, the goal of AI is to make life easier by handling tasks and solving problems for us. So, whether you're using a voice assistant like Siri or asking Google for directions, you've already experienced the benefits of AI — pretty neat, right?

How Does AI Work?

Think of AI as a very advanced version of your old household appliances. Remember your washing machine? You give it instructions, and it knows what to do. AI is similar but has a special twist: it can learn and get better over time.

For example, let's say you often ask your phone to find the nearest coffee shop. At first, it gives you a few options, but after a while, it starts to understand your preferences — maybe you prefer a place with good parking or a cozy spot with comfy chairs. It's like teaching your washing machine to get better at washing your favorite sweater every time you use it. The more you interact with AI, the more it learns what you like and adjusts to fit your needs.

Why Should You Care About AI?

You might be thinking, "This sounds interesting, but why does it matter to me?" Well, AI can actually help make your life a bit easier in practical ways:

- **Personalized Recommendations:** Have you ever noticed that Netflix suggests movies you might like or that your online shopping app recommends items that fit your style? That's AI at work, learning from your preferences and helping you discover new things you might enjoy.

- **Simplifying Everyday Tasks:** From setting reminders with your voice assistant ("Hey Siri, remind me to take my medication at 9 AM") to helping you find answers quickly on Google, AI acts like a helpful companion that's ready whenever you need it.

What Are Some Examples of AI in Your Life?

You might be surprised to learn just how often you're already using AI without even realizing it. Here are a few examples you might recognize:

- **Voice Assistants:** If you've ever asked Alexa, Siri, or Google Assistant a question, you've used AI. These assistants can answer questions, set timers, play your favorite songs, and even tell you the weather.

- **Navigation Apps:** Apps like Google Maps and Waze use AI to help you find the fastest route, taking traffic conditions into account. They learn from other drivers' data to give you the best directions possible.

- **Spam Filters:** Your email's spam filter uses AI to recognize and move unwanted emails out of your inbox. It learns from patterns and user feedback to get better at spotting junk mail.

Final Thoughts: Don't Be Afraid of AI

The world of AI can seem a bit futuristic, but at its core, it's here to assist us and make life easier. Remember, it's not about taking over — it's about helping out. Just like a good helper, AI is constantly improving based on your needs and feedback.

The next chapter will introduce you to some specific AI tools you might find helpful in your daily life. Keep in mind that AI is a fast-evolving field, so new updates and features are always coming out. But don't worry — I'll be here to help you make sense of it all. And remember, there's no rush to learn everything at once. We'll take it one step at a time, together.

So go ahead and give it a try! Ask your voice assistant a question, or notice the personalized recommendations in your apps. You're already using AI more than you might realize, and with a little practice, you'll feel right at home with these helpful tools.

Making AI Your New Best Friend

A Friendly Introduction to ChatGPT, Writing Helpers, and More

In recent years, some incredible new AI tools have emerged, making our lives a little easier and a lot more fun. Let's take a look at a few of these tools and how they can help you. Don't worry—you don't need to be a tech expert to enjoy them!

ChatGPT and Other AI Chatbots

One of the most exciting AI tools out there is **ChatGPT**, a type of chatbot designed to have a conversation with you, answer your questions, and even help you with writing. Think of it as a helpful, friendly companion who's always ready to brainstorm ideas, write a letter, or explain something in plain English.

What Can ChatGPT Do? You can ask ChatGPT almost anything. Whether you need help writing an email, want a recipe for dinner tonight, or feel curious about learning more about gardening, travel, or history, ChatGPT can offer answers, suggestions, and even some creative ideas during a friendly conversation. It's like having a personal assistant who never gets tired (or needs a coffee break!).

How to Use It: To get started with ChatGPT, simply visit a website like chat.openai.com on your computer, tablet, or even smartphone. There's also an official OpenAI app you can download on iOS or Android. Just type your question or request into the chat box, and ChatGPT will respond right away. Imagine chatting with a well-read friend who knows a bit about almost everything (but without interrupting you!).

Why It's Helpful: ChatGPT is great for getting quick answers without sifting through multiple websites. If you're not sure where to begin with writing tasks—like crafting a letter or starting a poem—ChatGPT can give you a helpful nudge in the right direction. Plus, it's available anytime you need a hand, day or night.

Grandson's Tip: Don't be afraid to experiment! When my grandma first tried ChatGPT, she asked it to recommend cookie recipes every day for a week. It was a fun way to get comfortable using the tool (and we ended up with some delicious cookies, too!).

AI Writing Assistants

Another fantastic AI tool is the **AI writing assistant**. These programs can help you write emails, documents, and even greeting cards for special occasions. If you ever get stuck searching for the right words, an AI writing assistant can make suggestions to help your writing flow more smoothly.

How It Works: To use an AI writing assistant, start by typing a few words about what you want to say. For example, if you're writing a birthday message but can't find the right words, just type "birthday message for a friend," and the AI will suggest some ideas. It's like having a little writing buddy who never judges your spelling mistakes.

Where to Find Them: Many email programs and word processors now include built-in AI writing tools. For instance, **Google Docs** and **Microsoft Word** have features that suggest text as you type, helping you write more easily and save time.

Grandson's Tip: The next time you're writing an email or note, try using one of these AI tools for a bit of help. You might be surprised at how much faster the words come to you!

AI Tools for Learning and Entertainment

AI isn't just for practical tasks; it can also be a lot of fun and a great way to learn something new.

Learning New Skills: AI-powered apps can help you learn almost anything—from cooking to speaking a new language. **Duolingo**, for example, uses AI to make language learning fun and interactive. It's like having a patient tutor who doesn't mind if you need to repeat a word several times.

Creating Art and Music: Ever wished you could paint a picture or compose a song? AI tools like **DALL-E** can create artwork from your descriptions. Just imagine a sunset over a lake, and the AI can recreate it for you. There are also AI music tools that can help you create your own tunes or relax with personalized playlists.

Health and Wellness Support: AI can even help you stay healthy. There are apps like **Medisafe** that remind you to take your medication and tools like **Headspace** that guide you through meditation sessions. These apps are like having a gentle nudge when you need a reminder to take care of yourself.

Grandson's Tip: If you're feeling curious, ask an AI tool to create a picture of your favorite vacation spot. My grandpa did this, and it brought back wonderful memories of our family trip to the beach.

How AI Tools Can Make Your Life Easier

AI tools aren't just for tech experts—they're designed to be useful and simple for everyone, including you. Here's how they can help:

Simplifying Daily Tasks: AI assistants can help you keep track of appointments, send messages, and find information quickly. You won't need to navigate complex websites or apps, making your day a little smoother.

Staying Connected: Chatbots like ChatGPT can help you send thoughtful messages to friends and family. They can even suggest conversation starters, making it easier to stay in touch.

Learning at Your Own Pace: With AI-powered learning tools, you can pick up new hobbies or skills whenever you're ready. Whether it's trying a new recipe, practicing a language, or exploring art, you have a helpful guide by your side.

Getting Quick Answers: Instead of searching the internet and sorting through a lot of information, you can ask an AI chatbot for direct answers. It's like having a personal librarian who knows exactly where to find what you need.

Grandson's Tip: When in doubt, start small. Ask a chatbot something simple, like "What's a good recipe for dinner tonight?" It's a great way to ease into using these tools and see how they can make your life easier.

Tips to Get Started with AI Tools

Getting started with AI might seem a bit intimidating, but it's easier than you think. Here are a few simple tips:

1. **Start with Easy Questions:** Try asking a chatbot something fun, like "Tell me a joke," or "Show me a picture of a dog." It's a lighthearted way to get comfortable.

2. **Try AI Writing Helpers:** The next time you're writing a note or an email, type a few words and see what suggestions come up. It's like having a co-writer who helps you find the right words.

3. **Use AI for Fun:** Remember, AI can be entertaining too! Ask it to recommend a new hobby, or describe a picture you'd like to see. It's all about exploring and having a bit of fun.

4. **Don't Be Afraid to Experiment:** There's no right or wrong way to use these tools. If you make a mistake, it's okay! The more you play around, the more comfortable you'll get.

Final Thoughts

AI might sound complicated, but it's really here to make life simpler and more enjoyable. Whether you're writing a letter, learning a new skill, or just looking for something fun to do, these tools can help. So, take your time, ask a few questions, and see how AI can fit into your day-to-day life. You've got this, and remember—your digital grandson is here to help you every step of the way!

Wrapping Up

DIGITAL GRANDSON PRESS

Wrapping Up with Your Digital Grandson: A Friendly Tech Farewell

Encouragement, Tips, and Next Steps for Staying Confident in the Digital World

As we wrap up our journey through the world of technology, I hope you're feeling a bit more confident, a little less intimidated, and maybe even excited to keep exploring. Learning about technology can feel overwhelming at times, but you've taken the time to understand tools that can make your life easier, help you stay connected, and even add a little fun to your day. That's something to be truly proud of!

Reflecting on How Far We've Come

Think about how much technology has changed—remember rotary phones and TV antennas? It's amazing how far we've come! The good news is that as technology keeps evolving, there are always new ways to learn and helpful tools designed to make life simpler. And even as things change, this guide has given you the skills to find your own answers, whether it's searching Google or asking ChatGPT for help.

If you're ever looking for more updates or tips, just visit the Digital Grandson's Guide to Tech website at www.thedigitalgrandson.com. It's like having your tech-savvy grandchild just a click away, ready to help out whenever you need it.

Key Takeaways: Remember These Tips as You Continue Exploring

1. Stay Curious

Technology might seem complex at first, but it's all about being curious and taking small steps. You don't have to learn everything at once—start with what interests you, and have a little fun along the way. You've already made great progress!

2. You Are Not Alone

Whether you're setting up a new smartphone, browsing the internet, or trying out an AI tool, remember that making mistakes is part of the process. It's normal, and everyone does it—even the experts! There are plenty of resources to help you, both online and in your own circle of friends and family.

3. Practice Makes Progress

Every time you use your device, you're building your skills. It's like learning to bake a pie or play your favorite tune on the piano—it takes a bit of practice, but each small success brings you closer to feeling more confident. Celebrate those moments, like setting your first reminder or sending a photo to a loved one. These are all victories!

4. Ask for Help When You Need It

Just as you've leaned on this guide for some of the basics, don't hesitate to ask for help from friends, family, or even online communities. There are many friendly folks out there who are happy to offer a hand. And remember, the Digital Grandson's Guide website is always here for you, too.

Looking Forward: What's Next?

The world of technology is full of exciting new developments. There's always something new to learn, whether it's the latest AI tools that can help with everyday tasks, new ways to stay connected with friends and family, or fun gadgets to try out. You don't need to know it all—just enjoy the discovery process and learn at your own pace.

Grandson's Tip:
When my grandpa first tried using an AI art tool, he asked it to recreate his favorite vacation spot by the beach. It brought back wonderful memories and started a whole conversation about our family trips. Don't be afraid to try something new—it might lead to something delightful!

Technology Should Serve You

It's easy to feel overwhelmed when facing something new, but remember: technology is here to serve you, not the other way around. It's perfectly okay if things seem confusing at first—that's part of the learning experience. Each time you press a button, try a new app, or ask a question, you're gaining confidence and control. And that's what matters most.

Grandson's Tip:
Think of it like learning to ride a bike. At first, it's wobbly and uncertain, but with each try, you get a little steadier. Before you know it, you're cruising along without a second thought!

Final, Final Thoughts: Keep Exploring with Confidence

You've done an amazing job diving into the world of technology. I hope you're proud of what you've accomplished. The digital world is just another tool to help you enjoy life, connect with the people you care about, and discover new things. Take your time, stay curious, and remember—it's okay to ask questions and have fun along the way.

If you ever want to learn more, get updates, or just refresh your memory, the Digital Grandson's Guide to Tech website is always here for you. Think of it as a quick call to your tech-savvy grandson—just a click away when you need it.

**With love, patience, and plenty of tech support,
Your digital grandson**

Keep exploring, keep asking, and most importantly—keep being yourself. Here's to many more exciting adventures in the digital world, one click at a time!

The Digital Grandson's Tech Glossary: Your Friendly Guide to Tech Terms

Simple Explanations and Helpful Tips for Navigating the Digital World with Confidence

Welcome to Your Tech Glossary!

Learning new technology can feel a bit like learning a new language, especially with so many unfamiliar words. But don't worry—you're not alone! This glossary is here to help. Whenever you come across a term you don't recognize, simply look it up here for a quick and friendly explanation. Think of it as your trusty guidebook, always ready to make your journey with technology a little easier. And remember, it's okay to take your time—learning is all about taking small steps forward. You've got this!

Activity Monitor: A tool on MacBooks that shows you what apps are running and how much energy they are using—great for troubleshooting.

AirDrop: A quick and easy way to share files between Apple devices without needing an internet connection, like sending a digital postcard.

Airplane Mode: A setting on your smartphone that turns off wireless connections like Wi-Fi, cellular, and Bluetooth. It's useful for saving battery or when you're on a plane.

Alexa: Amazon's voice-activated assistant, used in Echo devices. Alexa can help with tasks like playing music, setting reminders, providing weather updates, or controlling smart home gadgets—just by asking.

Amazon Appstore: An app store created by Amazon, similar to Google Play or Apple's App Store, where you can download apps for your devices.

Amazon Echo: A smart speaker created by Amazon, which uses Alexa to answer questions, play music, control smart home devices, and more.

Amazon Fire TV: A device that lets you stream movies, shows, and other content from the internet directly to your television.

Amazon Prime Video: A streaming service included with Amazon Prime. It offers movies, TV shows, and Amazon originals that you can watch online.

Amazon Prime: A subscription service that provides benefits like free shipping on many products, access to streaming movies and shows, and more. It's like getting VIP treatment for your shopping.

Amazon: An online shopping platform that started as a bookstore and quickly grew into one of the largest e-commerce sites in the world. You can buy almost anything on Amazon, and they'll ship it right to your door.

Antivirus Software: A program designed to protect your computer from harmful software (malware) that could steal your information or damage your device. It's like having a guard dog for your computer, keeping it safe from intruders.

App Store/Play Store: The marketplace on your smartphone where you can download new apps. The App Store is for iPhones, while the Google Play Store is for Android devices.

App: A software application that you can download to your smartphone or tablet. Apps are designed for specific purposes, like navigation (Google Maps), shopping (Amazon), or social networking (Facebook).

Apple ID: Your personal account used to access all Apple services, like the App Store, iCloud, and FaceTime. It's like your key to the Apple world.

Apple Maps: A GPS and navigation app developed by Apple, used to get directions and find places of interest.

Apple Music: A music streaming service available on MacBooks, allowing you to listen to millions of songs without needing to purchase each one.

Apple Pay: A digital wallet service that allows you to make payments using your Apple devices without needing physical credit or debit cards.

Apple Pencil: A stylus designed to work with iPads, allowing for precise drawing and writing, great for creative tasks or taking notes.

Apple Silicon: Apple's own processors used in newer MacBooks, providing better performance and battery life compared to older models.

Apple Store: The place where you can purchase Apple products, apps, and accessories, either online or in physical retail stores.

Apple Watch: A smartwatch that pairs with your iPhone, helping you track your health, receive notifications, and even make calls.

Apple: A technology company known for creating easy-to-use consumer electronics like iPhones, iPads, and Mac computers. Apple products are designed to make everyday tasks like communication, browsing, and entertainment simpler and more enjoyable.

AppleCare: An extended warranty program from Apple that provides additional support and repairs for your MacBook.

Bluetooth: A wireless technology used to connect devices over short distances, like connecting your phone to wireless headphones or a speaker.

Browser: A program used to access and navigate the internet, such as Google Chrome, Safari, or Firefox.

Buffering: When a video pauses while it's loading more data to play smoothly. It's a bit like waiting for the rest of a page in a book to be printed while you're reading it.

Cache: A storage location on your device that keeps data from websites and apps to help them load faster next time you use them.

Cart: A virtual shopping cart where you add items you want to buy while browsing an online store. It's just like using a cart in a physical store to hold all your items before you check out.

Checkout: The process of reviewing your selected items, entering your payment information, and completing your purchase. Think of it like getting in line at a store's register—just online.

Cloud Storage: A way to save data and files on remote servers that you can access from any device with an internet connection.

Command Key: A key on the MacBook keyboard used in combination with others to perform shortcuts, similar to the Control key on Windows.

Comment: A response to a post or photo that you can type out. It allows you to share your thoughts or interact with the content.

Confirmation Email: An email sent to you after making an online purchase, which includes the details of your order and confirmation that it was received.

Cortana: Cortana is Microsoft's voice-activated assistant, created to help you perform tasks, set reminders, and get answers to questions—just by speaking. You can think of Cortana as your digital helper, designed to make using your computer a bit easier and more fun.

Desktop: A computer that is designed to stay in one place, often found on desks. It usually has a separate monitor, keyboard, and mouse, and is great for working at home.

Device: An electronic tool like a smartphone, tablet, or computer that helps you interact with digital content.

Digital: Refers to anything involving computers, electronics, or the internet. It's like the difference between a paper photo and a picture on your phone—the digital version is the one you see on your screen.

Direct Message (DM): A private message you can send to someone on social media. Unlike comments, DMs are just between you and the person you're messaging.

Do Not Disturb: A setting on MacBooks that silences notifications so you can focus on work or relax without interruptions.

Dock: The bar at the bottom of the MacBook screen that shows your favorite apps for easy access, similar to a quick launch bar.

Download: The process of transferring data or software from the internet to your device.

FaceTime: An app on MacBooks that lets you make video calls to friends and family who also use Apple devices. It's like having a video chat built right in.

File: A collection of data stored on your computer, like a document or a photo. Think of it as a digital folder that holds information you need.

Finder Tags: Labels you can add to files and folders on your MacBook to make it easier to organize and search for documents.

Finder: A feature on MacBooks that helps you locate files, folders, and apps. It's like the file manager for all your documents.

Fingerprint Recognition: A security feature that uses your fingerprint to unlock a device or authorize a transaction.

Folder: A way to organize multiple files, similar to how you'd use a physical folder to keep papers together. It helps keep your computer neat and tidy.

Follower: Someone who subscribes to your social media account to see your posts and updates. It's like having a group of friends who want to stay in touch with what you're sharing.

Force Quit: A way to close an app that's not responding on your MacBook, similar to ending a task on a PC. It helps when an app gets stuck.

Gmail: An email service created by Google, which lets you send and receive messages. It's one of the most popular email platforms in the world.

Google Assistant: A voice-activated assistant by Google that helps you perform tasks, answer questions, and control smart home devices with simple voice commands.

Google Chrome: A web browser developed by Google that lets you explore the internet. It's known for being fast and easy to use.

Google Drive: A cloud storage service that allows you to store, share, and access your files from any device with an internet connection.

Google Maps: A navigation app that provides directions for driving, walking, cycling, and public transportation. It also helps you find local businesses and points of interest.

Google Photos: A photo storage service that automatically backs up your pictures and videos, making them easy to find and share.

Google: A technology company best known for its search engine, which helps you find information on the internet. Google also creates other helpful products and services.

GPS (Global Positioning System): A satellite-based navigation system that helps determine your exact location and provides directions to your destination.

Handoff: A feature that lets you start a task on one Apple device, like writing an email, and continue it on another, such as your MacBook.

Hard Drive: The main storage device in your computer where all your files, apps, and data are stored. It's like the brain of your computer that remembers everything.

Home Button: A button found on many smartphones that takes you back to the main screen, just like the 'home' key on an old phone.

Hub: A device that serves as a central control point for other smart devices. A smart speaker, like Amazon Echo, can act as a hub for your smart home.

Hulu: A streaming service that offers TV shows, movies, and live television. It's great for catching up on episodes of your favorite shows.

iCloud: Apple's cloud storage service that helps you save photos, files, and other data online so you can access it from any of your devices.

Install: The process of adding an app or program to your device so you can use it.

Internet Connection: The service that allows your device to connect to the web, enabling you to browse websites, use apps, and communicate online.

Internet: The internet is like a giant web that connects computers all around the world. It allows you to access information, watch videos, send emails, and connect with people, no matter where they are.

iPad: A tablet developed by Apple, used for activities like browsing the internet, watching videos, and reading.

iPhone: A smartphone by Apple that combines calling, texting, apps, and internet browsing in one device.

Keychain: A password manager built into macOS that helps you store and manage your passwords securely, making it easier to log in to websites.

Kindle: Amazon's e-reader device that lets you download and read books electronically. It's like carrying an entire library in your bag without the weight.

Laptop: A portable computer that you can take with you. It's like having a desktop that you can carry around and use anywhere—perfect for when you want flexibility.

Launchpad: A feature that shows all of your installed apps in one place, similar to a home screen on a smartphone, for easy access.

Like: On social media platforms, a 'Like' is a way to show that you appreciate a post, photo, or video. It's a simple way to give a virtual thumbs-up.

MacBook Air: A lighter, more portable MacBook, great for everyday tasks like browsing the web, emailing, and streaming.

MacBook Pro: A more powerful version of the MacBook, often used for professional work like graphic design, video editing, or programming.

MacBook: A laptop computer made by Apple. It combines sleek design with user-friendly features, making it great for both work and play.

macOS: The operating system used by Mac computers, similar to how Windows works on PCs. It's what makes your MacBook run smoothly.

Magic Keyboard: Apple's wireless keyboard, known for its comfortable typing experience and compatibility with MacBooks.

Magic Mouse: A wireless mouse made by Apple that works with MacBooks, featuring a smooth, multi-touch surface for gestures.

MagSafe: A special power connector used by some MacBooks. It easily snaps into place and releases if pulled, preventing accidents.

Malware: Malware is harmful software that can sneak onto your device and cause trouble, like stealing information or slowing things down. It's kind of like those pesky weeds in a garden—they're unwanted and can be a real nuisance. Antivirus software helps keep malware away and protects your device.

Mission Control: A feature on MacBooks that shows all open windows and apps, making it easier to switch between tasks.

Navigation: The act of planning and following a route to get from one place to another, often using a GPS device or app.

Netflix: A popular streaming service that allows you to watch a variety of TV shows, movies, and documentaries. Think of it like a giant library of entertainment, available anytime you want.

Notification Bar: A section at the top of your smartphone screen that shows updates, messages, and alerts from your apps.

Notification: A pop-up alert on your device that informs you about updates, messages, or reminders from your apps.

Offline Maps: Maps that you can download to your device and use without an internet connection.

Online Shopping: Purchasing items from a website or app without having to visit a physical store. Products are delivered to your doorstep.

Operating System: The software that runs your computer and allows all the other programs to work. Common ones are Windows for PCs and macOS for Apple computers—think of it as the boss that tells the computer how to do its job.

Passcode: A series of numbers or a pattern that you use to unlock your smartphone. It's like a digital key to keep your information safe.

Payment Method: The way you choose to pay for a purchase, such as using a credit card, debit card, or digital wallet.

Personalize: Customizing settings to fit your preferences, such as adjusting the volume of your smart speaker or selecting your favorite music service.

Playlist: A collection of songs or videos that you can create and play in order. It's like making your own personalized mixtape, but for digital content.

Preview: An app on MacBooks that allows you to view and edit PDFs and images without needing additional software.

QR Code: A square barcode that can be scanned with your device's camera to open a website, download an app, or access information.

Reboot: Turning your computer off and back on again to help solve problems or apply updates. It's like giving your computer a fresh start.

Recovery Mode: A special startup mode for troubleshooting your MacBook, used to reinstall macOS or fix system issues.

Reminder: A notification set through your smart speaker or app to help you remember tasks, such as watering the plants or taking medication.

Retina Display: A type of high-resolution screen used in MacBooks that makes text and images look incredibly sharp and clear, almost like looking at a printed photo.

Return Policy: The rules set by an online store about returning purchased items. It tells you how long you have to return something, what items are eligible, and whether you'll get a refund or store credit.

Router: A device that connects your devices to the internet and allows them to communicate with each other wirelessly.

Safari: The default web browser on MacBooks. It's where you go to browse the internet, similar to Google Chrome or Firefox.

Satellite: A device in space that sends signals to GPS devices on Earth, helping determine your location.

Screen Timeout: A setting that controls how long your device stays on without activity before the screen turns off to save battery.

Shipping Address: The address where you want your purchased items delivered. It's important to double-check this so your package ends up at the right doorstep!

Sidecar: A feature that lets you use an iPad as a second screen for your MacBook, adding more screen space for multitasking.

Siri: Siri is Apple's voice-activated assistant, designed to help you do things like send messages, set reminders, or get answers to questions—just by asking. Siri can be found on Apple devices like iPhones, iPads, and the Apple Watch. Think of Siri as your helpful, virtual personal assistant.

Smart Home: A home equipped with smart devices, like speakers, lights, and thermostats, that can be controlled remotely using a smartphone or voice commands.

Smart Speaker: A voice-activated speaker that can play music, answer questions, control smart home devices, and more. Examples include Amazon Echo and Google Home.

Spotlight: A built-in search tool on MacBooks that helps you quickly find apps, documents, and other information. It's like having a super-fast digital assistant.

Streaming Service: A platform that lets you watch movies, TV shows, or listen to music online without needing to download anything. Examples include Netflix, Amazon Prime Video, Hulu, and Spotify.

Streaming: Watching or listening to content (like TV shows, music, or movies) directly from the internet without needing to download it.

Subscription: A recurring payment that gives you access to a service, like Netflix or Hulu. It's like joining a club where you pay a monthly fee to enjoy the content.

System Preferences: The settings area on your MacBook where you can adjust things like display, sound, and internet connections.

Tag: Mentioning someone in a post or photo by using the '@' symbol followed by their name. It's like giving someone a shout out to get their attention.

Taskbar: A bar that appears on your screen (usually at the bottom) that helps you switch between different programs and see what's open. Think of it like the remote control for your computer.

Thunderbolt Port: A high-speed connection port on MacBooks used for connecting accessories like external monitors or hard drives.

Time Machine: A backup feature on MacBooks that helps you create backups of your files, so you don't lose important data if something goes wrong.

Touch Bar: A strip of touch-sensitive buttons on some MacBook Pros that change based on the app you're using, providing quick shortcuts.

Touch ID: A fingerprint sensor on some MacBooks that allows you to unlock your device or make purchases securely with just a touch.

Touchscreen: The screen on your smartphone that responds to your touch. It's how you interact with apps, type messages, and navigate your device.

Tracking Number: A number provided by the shipping company that lets you track where your package is during delivery. It's like having a little map that shows your package's journey to your door.

Trackpad: The flat, touch-sensitive surface below the keyboard on a MacBook that you use to move the cursor and click, like a mouse.

Turn-By-Turn Directions: Step-by-step navigation instructions provided by GPS apps, guiding you on how to get to your destination.

Update: Installing the latest version of an app or software to get new features or fix problems.

USB Cable: A type of cable used to connect devices for charging or transferring data.

Voice Command: A spoken instruction that your smart speaker or GPS app can understand and respond to, such as "Play music" or "Get directions to the nearest gas station."

Wallpaper: The background image on your computer's desktop. You can personalize it with a photo of your choice, just like hanging a favorite picture in your room.

Waze: A GPS app known for providing real-time traffic updates, based on information shared by other drivers.

Website: A website is like a digital home on the internet where you can find information, shop, watch videos, or connect with others. Think of it like a library or store, but online.

Wi-Fi: A technology that allows devices to connect to the internet wirelessly. Wi-Fi is needed for most smart home devices and online activities.

Window: A framed area on your computer screen where a program is displayed. Just like a real window lets you see outside, a digital window lets you see different parts of a program.

Zoom: A feature that allows you to enlarge or shrink a view on your screen, useful when you need to see map details more clearly. It is also a video conferencing app.

Closing Note

This glossary is your handy tech companion. Keep it close by, and don't hesitate to refer to it whenever you need a little extra help. Remember, learning something new is all about taking one step at a time—and you're doing an amazing job. If you ever need more explanations or want extra tips, just visit www.thedigitalgrandson.com. I'm always here to help, like a tech-savvy grandchild who's just a click away!

With love, patience, and a little bit of tech magic,
Your Digital Grandson

About The Digital Grandson's Guide to Tech

Who We Are, What We Offer, and How We're Here to Help You Every Step of the Way

The Digital Grandson's Guide to Tech is here to make technology simple, accessible, and—most importantly—useful for you. We know that learning new tech can feel a bit overwhelming at times, but it doesn't have to be. Think of us as your patient, tech-savvy grandchild, sitting down with you to guide you step by step. Whether you're figuring out your smartphone or setting up a smart home, we'll keep things clear, straightforward, and maybe even a little fun along the way.

Here's What We Offer, All Designed with You in Mind:

- **Easy-to-Follow Tutorials:** Clear, step-by-step guides that help you tackle everyday tech tasks without frustration. We break things down into simple steps, so you can follow along at your own pace.

- **Guide Books:** Handy resources like this one, perfect for keeping on your bookshelf as a trusty reference whenever you need a little help.

- **Helpful Newsletters:** Stay in the loop with our monthly tips and recommendations. We keep things brief and practical, so you can stay informed without feeling overwhelmed.

You'll find even more free resources, tutorials, and a welcoming community on our website: www.thedigitalgrandson.com. It's like having your tech-savvy grandchild just a click away—always ready to lend a hand, whether you need a quick tip or want to dive deeper into something new.

Grandson's Tip:
If you ever feel stuck, remember it's okay to take a break and come back when you're ready. Learning takes time, and you're doing great just by being here.

Keep Exploring and Keep Asking Questions

Remember, technology is just a tool, and we're here to help you make the most of it. Don't hesitate to reach out if you need help—that's what we're here for! You've got this, and we're right by your side every step of the way.

**With love, patience, and plenty of tech support,
The Digital Grandson's Guide Team**

Made in United States
North Haven, CT
20 March 2025